LIFE IN
ELIZABETHAN ENGLAND

A rich Elizabethan lady at her dressing-table
From a portrait of Elizabeth Vernon, Countess of Southampton

Life in
ELIZABETHAN
ENGLAND

A. H. DODD

English Life Series
Edited by PETER QUENNELL

Capricorn Books
NEW YORK: G. P. PUTNAM'S SONS

SBN: 399–50298–X
Library of Congress Catalog
Card Number 73–84468

Reprinted with the permission of B. T. Batsford, Ltd.

G. P. PUTNAM'S SONS
200 Madison Avenue, New York 16, N.Y.

To

Mary, Elisabeth, Ruth

and Sara

Contents

Acknowledgment

The author wishes to record his appreciation of the great help given to him by the Librarian and staff of the National Library, Aberystwyth, and of University College Library, Bangor.

The illustration on page 6 is reproduced by gracious permission of Her Majesty the Queen, from a MS. in the Royal Library, Windsor.

The author and publishers also wish to thank the following for permission to reproduce the other illustrations appearing in this book:

The Ashmolean Museum, Oxford, for the illustration on page 104 (top); the Trustees of the British Museum for pages 5, 12, 15, 22–24, 30, 36, 37, 41, 44, 47, 60, 65, 75, 83, 85, 86, 88, 90, 94, 96, 104 (bottom), 105, 109, 116, 127, 131, 132, 139, 141, 156, 159, 161, 164 and 165; the Duke of Buccleuch and Queensberry, K.T., G.C.V.O. for the frontispiece; the Courtauld Institute for page 144; Simon Wingfield Digby for page 13; Fiske-Moore Studios for page 89; Kinistil Photos for pages 56 and 103; the National Library of Wales for pages 31 and 32; the Director and Trustees of the National Maritime Museum for page 158; the National Portrait Gallery for pages 69, 71 and 119; B. Payne for page 50; Dr J. K. St Joseph (Crown Copyright Reserved) for page 28; the Marquis of Salisbury for page 68; the Librarian, University College of North Wales, Bangor, for page 50; the Trustees of the Victoria and Albert Museum for pages 4 and 124; Sir R. Williams-Bulkeley for page 50.

List of Illustrations

xi

LIST OF ILLUSTRATIONS

xiii

I

Kingdom, Queen and Court

The first Elizabethan age, as we are pleased nowadays to call it, has an inner unity, a distinctive character of its own marking it off sharply from most of the 'periods' into which history is conveniently (but often arbitrarily) divided. The change in atmosphere makes itself felt at the very outset, and the characteristic aura lingers on thinly into the next reign until the last of the great Elizabethans has gone. The whole age is coloured by the rich personality of the queen herself, but never swamped by it: one of her triumphs was the active response she drew from a wide range of social levels and geographical areas, making her reign equally an age of the ordinary Englishman. For what elicited the response was devotion not so much to the abstract concept of England as to a living person, seen through a haze of romance yet decidedly human and accessible.

Naturally unity was never a hundred per cent, or anything like it. There were always cross-currents, now barely agitating the surface, now muddying the stream till its course and direction are almost lost to sight. The climax came when, after two decades of uncertainty, the country's independence was threatened by the might of a world-wide empire and the still potent thunders of the spiritual head of Christendom. This second line of attack might have proved fatal to unity had not the first provoked the patriotic reaction of a nation with its back to the wall. It was all in a different key from Creçy and Agincourt, where English national consciousness came to birth; there was little of the spirit of conquest or foreign adventure in the Elizabethan call to action, least of all in the mind of the

1

queen herself. But the threat was such as to rally behind the throne the bulk of those who would otherwise have been most sensitive to orders from Rome, and to throw waverers into the arms of the minority of whole-hogging protestants. Patriotism in this way gained a new religious sanction and fervour. The 'fifth column' which was prepared to hail the king of Spain as champion of the faith and to pray for the success of his Armada was very thinly represented at home; it was only among the small band of religious exiles, and by no means universally there, that men could be found to go all the way with priest Joseph Cresswell: 'If I heard that the entire destruction of England was for the greater glory of God and the welfare of Christianity, I should be glad of its being done.'

Here then was an atmosphere favourable both materially and psychologically to great creative achievements. The booty that kept pouring into the country for some half-dozen years after the Armada's defeat not only enriched the few but diffused a wider prosperity. London was replacing Antwerp as the financial capital of northern Europe. English armies may have failed to repeat, against a far more formidable military machine, the triumphs of the Hundred Years War; but the English navy— a new phenomenon—more than once proved itself a match for all comers, and English seamen were catching up with and even surpassing the Spanish and Portuguese pioneers of oceanic exploration. The English language had not yet won the currency abroad of English sterling, but at home the broadcasting of the English Bible was creating a public steeped in its idiom, and so preparing what had ranked as an obscure *patois* for an international status worthy of its growing power and flexibility. Meanwhile events were shaking Englishmen out of the insularity which had been the price of seclusion from catholic Europe, and since their language would not, as nowadays, carry them everywhere, they had to undergo the healthy discipline of meeting the foreigner on his own ground; the country was beginning to breed proficient modern linguists.

The devotion and self-confidence engendered by these years of peril helped to carry England across the trough of the wave in the last decade of the reign, when Spain had learned to

counter our buccaneering tactics, booty ceased to flow in, and war taxation and bad harvests were lowering everyone's spirits. The dream of finally smashing Spanish naval power and replacing her in the lordship of the world faded away. The queen had never shared the enthusiasm of her admirals for so ambitious a war-aim, and it went under with Drake and Hawkins in 1596. Then again increasing persecution of those whose religious dissidence threw doubts on their political loyalty put a heavy strain on the new-found national unity, and created a climate in which a restless spirit like Essex could rally round him

The Queen in state

a motley following of malcontents. Yet it was now that English drama reached maturity, and that the challenge of poverty was met by a great constructive effort, not indeed towards the establishment of a Welfare State (no one had yet dreamed that up, unless it were More in his *Utopia*), but at least of a modest National Minimum. If the reign did not end in a blaze of glory, its sunset glow lit up an abundant and lasting harvest.

And the achievements of the age were emphatically national achievements, not just those of a small band of exceptionally gifted statesmen, creative artists or men of action isolated from the masses. The exploits of Drake and Hawkins were possible because their strategic and organising genius could use the widening experience and hardihood of the common seaman on his lawful (and unlawful) occasions. It was not only intellectuals inspired by the continental Renaissance who created the Shakesperian drama, the Elizabethan madrigal or the Tudor manor house: without folk traditions to build upon and habitual

A miniature of the Queen

playgoers and fireside singers to appeal to, the work of the great masters might have been as isolated as the English of *Euphues,* and the gulf which grew in the next century between the *intelligentsia* and the masses might have been anticipated. As it was, learned and simple were still able to understand each other, and class barriers in education were far from insurmountable—to the great enrichment of national life. The Reformation itself could hardly have withstood the shocks of the age if its sole support had been the learning of theologians and the schemes of policy-makers; but it had a broader basis in the aspirations and spiritual experiences of simple Bible-readers who read little else. The Elizabethan Poor Law, again, was not just a bright idea of master-planners, but an outcome of the practical experience of harassed municipalities and the charity of enlightened philanthropists from many grades of society. Even in the field of knowledge where the reign had least to show—that of natural science—we note how the lore of the English countryside is absorbed into the stream of botanical science when John Gerard catalogues his plants under their common country names alongside the botanist's Latin.

On a different plane, much the same might be said of the queen's success in completing her father's work of absorbing the Welsh into the wider British community without pulling up their cultural roots. This was largely due to the co-operation of Welsh scholars and patriots in translating the Bible and Prayer Book; and of course the queen's own Welsh antecedents stood her in good stead. Unhappily they could not help her to solve the far thornier problem of Ireland; this legacy of acute disunion she passed on to her successors, who fared no better. But at least the way had been prepared for union with Scotland: Great Britain was on its way.

This brings us back to the queen herself and the court she gathered around her. That she was able to inspire such divers elements with a common devotion and purpose was due in part to gifts of personality which persistently elude analysis, in part to the fact that she had the mind and the education to appreciate the broader currents of contemporary culture without losing the common touch which bound her to her subjects, with all their traditions and prejudices. In this way we escaped the danger of a brilliant court insulated from an apathetic public. So the court forms a natural starting-point for a study of the age.

The Queen gives audience

A young courtier, doubtfully identified as Sir Philip Sidney
From a miniature by Isaac Oliver, c. 1590

Contempt for courts and courtiers was a stock theme of Elizabethan literature.

> *Hath not old custom made this life more sweet*
> *Than that of painted pomp? Are not these woods*
> *More free from peril than the envious court?*

demands Duke Senior in *As You Like It*; and Antony Munday answers the rhetorical question in 'The woodman's walk':

> *My first day's walk was to the court,*
> *Where beauty fed mine eyes:*
> *Yet found I that the courtly sport*
> *Did mask in sly disguise.*
> *For falsehoods sat in fairest looks*
> *And friend to friend was coy;*
> *Court favour fill'd but empty books*
> *And there I found no joy.*

But Duke Senior shows no marked reluctance to return to the 'envious court' when his brother abdicates, nor do any of his courtiers, except the misanthropic Jaques; and there is no reason to believe that Munday—draper, actor, ballad-monger, playwright and above all adventurer with an eye to the main chance—would have spurned an *entrée* to Elizabeth's court, had opportunity knocked. How many Elizabethans would have chosen with Jaques the way of contemplation and sardonic detachment? For detached contemplation had gone out of fashion with the monks. In an age of rapid and exciting change, most men wanted to be in the swim, and what better vantage point for that than the royal court?

The Reverend William Harrison, whose acute if somewhat roseate descriptions of Elizabethan England form a fitting introduction to Holinshed's Chronicles, very properly disclaims any inner knowledge of the queen's court, 'sith my calling is, and hath been such, as that I have scarcely presumed to peep in at her gates'; this, of course, was before he became canon of Windsor, and so in a position to do more than 'peep in'. Yet he makes bold to claim that 'The court of England, which necessarily is holden always where the prince lieth, is in these days

7

Eltham Palace

one of the most renowned and magnificent courts that are to be found in Europe', exceptional only in its outward decorum. The good canon must have known even less about continental courts than he did about Elizabeth's; but there seems to have been some substance in his comparison. No Victorian dowager could have kept more vigilant watch over her charges than did Elizabeth over her maids of honour, as even the mostly highly placed of her courtiers found to their cost. For offending in this regard Ralegh himself forfeited the leadership of an expedition to the Indies for which he had advanced most of the capital, and he was released from prison only just in time to recover less than his due share of the booty.

It was a gay and colourful court for all that. A Dutch diplomat visiting Eltham Palace when Sir Christopher Hatton was keeper there swore that in all his travels through France, Italy and Spain he had never met the equal of its instrumental music, its pack of greyhounds for the chase, or the rich accoutrements of its horsemen. Eltham was a palace rarely visited; but the queen had a dozen others on which she could ring the changes. Christmas, a round of masques and other dazzling spectacles, was usually kept at Whitehall. But apart from special seasons there was gaiety and colour enough in the daily or weekly processions from Chapel to Presence Chamber, from Presence Chamber to Privy Chamber, from Privy Chamber to Withdrawing Chamber, or, more at large, by water from Greenwich to Whitehall or in cavalcade from Whitehall to Windsor, with knots of onlookers kneeling as the queen passed by. Wherever she went there was dancing, for the queen loved it to the end of her life. Nor was court life all frivolity. We need not go all the way with Harrison when he assures us that 'the stranger that entereth into the court of England upon the

sudden shall rather imagine himself to come into some public
school of the universities, where many give ear to one that
readeth, than into a prince's palace, if you confer with those of

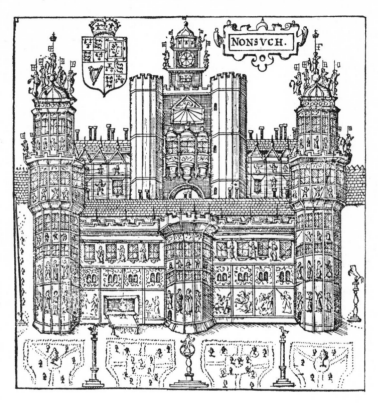

Nonesuch Palace, the Queen's favourite residence

other nations', and not even he suggests that the Bible, the
histories and chronicles and the other improving literature
which she left in every room were read and digested by all who
resorted to court. But when we recall the names of Elizabeth's
chief courtiers it is easy to accept his assurance that 'there are
very few of them which have not the use and skill of sundry

9

speeches, besides an excellent vein of writing beforetime not regarded', to say nothing of aptitude in music and poetry.

After all, the queen herself was a woman of many accomplishments. She could play the virginals or hold her own in wit and repartee with the best of them; she could address foreign ambassadors in Latin, French or Spanish—impromptu if need were; and the care with which she corrected her own speeches for publication shows an equal concern for 'English undefiled'. Obviously her courtiers could not allow themselves to be outshone by a 'weak and feeble woman', nor allow their own wives to cover them with shame by their *gaucherie*. One of the great achievements of the Renaissance, if not one of its causes, was the new diplomatic standard (first set by the Renaissance popes) whereby the prestige of a court, and thence of the country it represented, was measured in terms of scholarship as well as splendour: not for nothing was *orator* accepted as the Latin equivalent for 'ambassador'. In this the court of Elizabeth did not lag behind the standards of the age. Burghley was exceptional in confessing himself 'only meet to speak as my mother taught me'.

Then too the court was the hub of gossip—and gossip of a kind the whole country was agog to hear. Much, it is true, could be picked by merely strolling up and down the aisle of St. Paul's, where 'men of all professions not merely mechanic' were wont to forgather between eleven and noon and between three and six to pick up the news which some courtier or other could be relied on to blurt out. But this was only second-hand news, and it took the genius of a John Chamberlain to give it the eye-witness flavour of those inimitable news letters that delighted his friends for thirty years. Chamberlain was quite happy to be on the fringes. Men of more bustling temperament wanted their news hot: no less than the modern crowd that hangs about Downing Street in time of national crisis, they wanted to see with their own eyes who was downcast and who jubilant. It was 'curiosity rather than ambition' (so he himself declares) that took young Edward Herbert, the future Lord Herbert of Cherbury, to court at the age of eighteen or nineteen—but already a married man ('It is pity he was married so young', was the queen's

characteristic comment after she had enquired who the person-
able young courtier might be). It is wise, however, not to trust
too implicitly what Lord Herbert tells us about himself;
he liked to show himself as a man of fashion rather than a
man of serious purpose, and it is not easy to believe, in the light
of the constant pestering for public employment that occupied
so much of his later years, that he was indifferent to this aspect
of attendance at court.

Richmond Palace, another royal residence

Certainly not many of Elizabeth's courtiers were. Had not her
own grandfather's grandfather come to court as an obscure
Welsh country gentleman, with the further handicap that his
family had been kinsmen and supporters of the rebel Glyndŵr,
and there wooed and won the widow of Henry V? And had not
his son in turn used this standing at court to advantage by
marrying the heiress of the house of Lancaster, and so providing
the heir of the marriage, Elizabeth's grandfather, with a claim
on the throne itself? True, crowns were less easy to pick up
now that the Wars of the Roses were over, but there were other,
less glittering but still enviable prizes within the grasp of the
aspiring courtier. Thomas Myddelton, a future lord mayor and
(in contemporary values) millionaire, paid his first visit to
court, probably under Sir Francis Walsingham's wing, in 1585,

not long after his return from Antwerp as factor to a sugar firm. This led on to his appointment as collector of customs at the outports, a post which not only gave him capital with which to speculate, but introduced him to Hawkins, Drake, Frobisher and other leading seamen of the age, who admitted him to a share in financing their profitable raids on Spanish commerce. It was the booty acquired on these raids that set him on the highroad to fortune.

Harrison might have found here yet another point of contrast with foreign courts: in how many of them could a mere sugar factor have found such ready admission to the Presence Chamber? Elizabeth's was in a very real sense a popular court, and up to a point an epitome of England. It was the Stuarts who brought in the antithesis between court and country. At the very beginning of the queen's reign the Spanish ambassador, accustomed to a very different order, observed with a mixture of wonder and contempt how 'she is much attached to the people'. 'It pleaseth her in the summer season', Harrison tells us, 'to recreate herself abroad, and view the estate of the country, and hear the complaints of her commons injured by her unjust officers.' These were what Sir John Neale calls her summer holidays, when she carried the whole court with her from palace to palace and from royal manor to royal manor, or conferred on favoured subjects the costly honour of accepting their private hospitality. The progress was informal enough to make access to the sovereign easy for such as awaited her on the route or at the entrance to town or shire.

The Queen on progress, accompanied by the symbolic figure of Fame

On the other hand, of course, London knew her best, and next to London those shires of the south-east which were still for most purposes the effective England, and remained so till the Industrial

Procession of Queen Elizabeth to Blackfriars, 9th June 1600

Revolution. She never travelled farther north than Derby
or farther west than Bristol. There was talk of her visiting
Shrewsbury, and more than once of her visiting York, but it
never came to anything. The marches of north and west
were not yet fully within the pale of civilisation; just beyond
them lay the queen's ancestral Wales, where English law had
only held complete ascendancy for some twenty years, and
Scotland, an independent and always potentially hostile sovereign
state. Besides, each of these regions had its own viceregal court,
a replica of the queen's own court save that the queen herself
was absent and the lawyers (in view of its wide judicial
functions) present in force. But the president was usually a
local magnate, not a lawyer; he held his court, after a peri-
patetic phase in both areas, in a comparable setting: Ludlow
castle for the Welsh marches, and for the North a handsome
building at York constructed from the stones of St. Mary's
Abbey. Each tried to give his court something of the social
splendour and prestige that would attract thither the chief local
gentry as courtiers, not just as litigants. But the court at York,

13

Manor Palace, York, seat of the Council of the North

set in the midst of a largely disaffected gentry in a countryside kept a-simmer for nearly twenty years by their intrigues with a rival queen, had a bleaker and less sociable air than the court at Ludlow, where (in the words of a contemporary) 'a young man might have learned as much good behaviour and manners as should have stucke to him ever after whiles he lived'. At Ludlow all the gentry who counted in Wales and the marches were entertained with a round of banquets and masques not unworthy of Whitehall when they flocked there at Christmas to pay their respects and their Christmas gifts to the president; and a generation after the queen's death, following a period when in both courts the professional had gained on the courtly element, they might have witnessed there the first performance of Milton's *Comus*. York was not to know the gaiety of a court until Charles I came there on the eve of civil war—and then it was perforce a subdued gaiety.

Further Reading

(relevant also to ensuing chapters)

CONTEMPORARY

W. Camden, *Britannia* (ed. Gibson), 1695.

[Hales], *A Discourse of the Common Weal of this Realm of England* (ed. Lamond), 1893.

LATER

J. B. Black, *The Reign of Elizabeth*, second edition, 1959.

M. St. Clare Byrne, *Elizabethan Life in Town and Country* (illustrated), 1925.

Elizabethan Government and Society (ed. Bindoff, Hurstfield and Williams), 1961.

D. Harrison, *Tudor England*, Vol. II (illustrated), 1953.

Sir J. Neale, *Queen Elizabeth* (illustrated), 1934.

Allardyce Nicoll, *The Elizabethans* (illustrated), 1957.

A. L. Rowse, *The England of Elizabeth* (illustrated), 1950.

L. F. Salzman, *England in Tudor Times* (illustrated), 1926.

Shakespeare's England, two vols. (illustrated), 1916.

Social England (ed. Traill and Mann), Vol. III (illustrated), 1902.

G. M. Trevelyan, *Illustrated English Social History*, Vol. II, 1950.

D. Williams, *History of Modern Wales*, 1952.

*Ludlow Castle, residence of the President of
Wales and the Marches*

II

Country Life

Medieval England has been called a community of communities; Elizabethan England still retained something of that character. What the royal palace was to the country at large the aristocratic mansion and even the small country house were to the surrounding countryside. The great lord had his hierarchy of officials, his masques and balls, his Presence Chamber, his trumpeter and herald, his hunts and highdays and holidays, on a scale not unworthy of comparison with those of Whitehall or Hampton Court; his neighbours, great and small, came bearing their Christmas or New Year gifts, his tenants their tributes in cash or kind at quarter days, with something of the same pomp and circumstance. Every lord of the manor, however petty, had his own little parliament in the court leet, where his steward presided as speaker, and a jury of tenants—his 'faithful commons'—presented through him their grievances, laid down in their own miniature Acts of Parliament what regulations were needed for the village fields, or, where a town had not yet received its own charter of self-government, the town streets, and adjusted by immemorial custom—their local Common Law—disputes between neighbours.

This last was, of course, a function long since abandoned by the parliament at Westminster (save for its survival in private Acts) in favour of the law courts: but the fusion of legislation, administration and justice survived in the manor court long after it had been outgrown at Westminster. This can be illustrated by examples taken at random from the records, part Latin, part English, of a rural court leet during two decades of the reign. They show the lord's steward sitting at irregular intervals, with the assistance of a jury of six to twenty of the more substantial tenants of the manor, to hear reports

Some men and women of the country
1 *An archer*   2, 7 *Commoners*   3 *The Lord of the Manor*
4 *The Sheriff*   5 *A Rustic*   6 *The Lady of the Manor*

17

and complaints from the petty constable of each of its tiny townships, and issuing general orders on the upkeep of the stocks, pound, mills, archery butts, supplies of bows and arrows, or the observance of the law of 1571 enjoining the wearing of woollen caps every Sunday to help the wool trade. Fines are imposed, whether on individuals (including the parson) or on whole townships, for such offences as despoiling the woodland for fuel or house repairs, smuggling unauthorised cattle on to the common, allowing sheep, unringed pigs and above all the omnivorous goat to stray and to trample or devour other men's crops; or again for keeping unlicensed taverns, playing cards or skittles for money, or just for absence from court.

The sway of the manor courts was purely local; county affairs were in the hands of the county magistrates, appointed by the crown from among the principal landowners from all parts of the shire, so that where necessary they could act in twos and threes to deal with matters arising in their own hundreds or commotes. It was through these widely dispersed institutions that the ordinary Englishman was brought into contact in his daily affairs with the life of the wider community. To understand Elizabethan England, then, we must take our stand not at one single centre, but at scores of them—how many score we are reminded whenever we tramp the English countryside and see how thickly studded it is today with former manor houses, whether stately home, humble farmstead or mouldering ruin. They commonly carry an Elizabethan date or at least an Elizabethan porch or gatehouse or chimney, for hers was a great age of rebuilding. Greater security, greater wealth, new building fashions seen abroad, between them these created the will and the means to build new homes or to adapt and enlarge old ones with an eye to comfort and display instead of protection: except indeed in the restless north, where mosstroopers and border raids postponed this stage till after the union of the crowns. 'Sooner shall we see a gentleman build a stately house than give alms and cherish the needy', was one of the many charges brought against the gentry by contemporary moralists. Whether their building programmes did indeed affect their charities may be doubted; statistics

18

recently published show, on the contrary, a rising curve of charitable benefactions throughout the reign, with the gentry ranking high among the benefactors.

What it certainly did affect was their purses. 'What saie youe to oure buildinges, that we have heare in Inglond of late daies', asks the Knight

A typical half-timbered manor-house:
Old Moreton Hall, Cheshire

in Hales's contemporary *Discourse of the Common Weal*, 'far more excessive then at anie time heretofore; doth not that empoverishe the Realme, and cause men to kepe lesse howses?' To which the Doctor replies with the startlingly modern argument that although 'the buyldinge and trimminge of these howses spent awaie that that should otherwise be spent in howsehold', the realm as a whole gains in increased employment. Actually the money was more often raised by loan or mortgage, and by luck or good management in match-making or job-hunting, or by resort to business methods alien to the traditions of his order, the aspiring squire was generally able to meet his obligations, or at least to bequeath them to his posterity, without reducing his scale of living. But many of them were walking a financial tight-rope; perhaps it was but poetic justice that so often it was a later generation, in whose interests they had over-built themselves, that paid the penalty, when harder times came, by sinking in the social scale.

No wise man, however, will take his history from the moralists, of Elizabeth's age or any other. As an up-and-coming grade of society, the gentry became their principal targets almost as 'the poor' were to Victorian moralists—almost, but not quite; for of course the gentry could not be patronised. Not that either was a new phenomenon; but to contemporaries both showed signs of unhealthy growth marked by unfamiliar vices. Modern historians have been more interested in the material fortunes of the gentry than in their morals, but that has proved no easier matter for generalising at large. There can be no doubt that the social changes of the century preceding the queen's accession had produced a marked increase in the numbers of those who professed and called themselves gentry, lived as such and were so accepted by their neighbours. But to speak of the gentry as entering into the wea'th and influence of a decayed nobility would be a gross over-simplification.

The nobility were, in contemporary eyes like those of Harrison, themselves but an exalted sub-section of the gentry, divided from 'those that be no lords, as knight, esquires and simple gentlemen' by what Professor Trevor-Roper calls 'a distinction of nomenclature and legal rights, not a difference of either habits of mind or economic practice'.

Not that the distinction is without social importance. The hereditary character of the peerage gave the order a degree of permanence over and above that of the gentry at large, for a simple gentleman might 'lose his gentry' by mere extravagance, whereas a peer could lose his peerage only by conspicuous public misconduct. His exalted rank, and his membership of a legislative chamber which remained powerful for all the encroachments of the commons, gave him closer access to the royal ear. The 'distinction of nomenclature' meant that a somewhat more dignified 'port' was expected of him, for while the simple gentleman might live like a lord, the lord could not live like a simple gentleman without losing face; and the spirit of feudalism was still strong enough to make him a more likely choice for the leadership of armies or the new military office of lord

The country nobility

lieutenant in the shires—both of which in turn enhanced his local influence. Elizabeth, it is true, was sparing in her creations of new titles and, after her experience of aristocratic revolts, a little chary of aristocratic officers of state; but the so-called 'middle class' counsellors to whom she resorted were largely the sort of men her more expansive father would probably have elevated to the peerage. Yet the very limitation of numbers gave the peerage a scarcity value which James I's lavish creations were destined to undermine, for all his tendency to lean on the lords; and if the Elizabethan peer, unlike his opposite number in France, remained but a gentleman writ large, the writing was large enough to make him an imposing figure.

The gentry, then, were a broad and comprehensive section of society ranging from peers of the realm, through knights and esquires (who constituted, roughly speaking, the 'greater gentry') to those 'lesser gentry' who had only just raised themselves from the status of yeoman and were distinguished from it by differences in mode of address ('master' instead of 'goodman') rather than in economic status. To speak of them, or of any other 'degree' in Elizabethan society, in Marxian 'class' categories is to misread the essential character of Elizabethan England, where, in the words Miss Wedgwood uses of the following century, 'the dominating loyalties . . . were not class loyalties and interests, but local loyalties and interests within an accepted hierachy'. For this reason the question whether the gentry at large were on the up grade or the down grade in this age is wrongly posed. What is true of one district is false of another; and we shall need a good deal more detailed knowledge both of individual estates and of local variations before any really effective generalisation can be made.

For example, if your estate lay on or near one of the high-roads to London, with a constant stream of two-way traffic past your door on legal or administrative business or parliamentary affairs, you were far more likely than a mere back-woodsman to be in the swim of new political and religious developments, and by the same token to gain a start in the race for public office, on which so many landlords depended to bridge the gap between their rents and their expenditure.

The significance of the much-trodden ways that led through Wales to Elizabethan Ireland in the matter of religious conformity and its rewards is matched by their importance in the world of commerce. It is doubtful whether young Thomas Myddelton would ever have found his way to London and fortune had not his native Denbigh lain on what was then one of the principal ways to Ireland; it is certain that without that contact his relatives at home would never have been admitted to part shares, from £20 to a paltry 50s., in his privateering speculations, bringing them several hundred per cent return, in gold, on their outlay. Within their own limited spheres Plymouth, Bristol and the other seaports similarly spread the benefits of peaceful commerce and of buccaneering far and wide along their landward approaches. The 'northern parts' had to wait for the union of the crowns before there could be the same traffic in ideas, goods and jobs to the benefit of estates which bordered the Great North Road; but at least there was Newcastle, where London got its coal, to serve (in Dr. Trevelyan's words) as 'a meeting-point of the feudal world of the Percies, the tribal world of the mosstrooper, and the coal trade not fundamentally different from that of to-day'.

Ploughing

Below the gentry came the even more amorphous grade of yeoman. The legal definition of a yeoman as 'a freeholder that may dispend forty shillings per annum' was manifestly out of date by Elizabeth's day, for many of them were far richer than this (as witness their benefactions, which included Harrow school!), and many were not freeholders. The yeomanry has been rightly called a rural middle class, and like urban middle classes it lacked, even more than the gentry, any fixity of composition; it was in a perpetual state of flux, serving as a sort of half-way house to gentility. It would not be far from the truth to say that the basic

22

difference between gentleman and yeoman lay in expenditure rather than in income. The prosperous yeoman literally ploughed his profits back into the land, living heartily but plainly; the gentleman had to earmark much of his for keeping up what was due to his 'degree' in building, housekeeping, entertaining, and unpaid public duty. At the same time the fluid state of society in general, and the land market in particular, since the later middle ages, afforded boundless opportunities for the yeoman to 'become a squire' like that 'forkt radish with a head fantastically carved upon it', Master Shallow, whose

Ploughing, sowing and harrowing

low origins damned him in Falstaff's eyes equally with his meagre dimensions. It might be done by buying up neighbouring freeholds or land forfeited to the crown, with the proceeds of military service, of service in a noble or gentle household or merely of patient industry, on his own lands or on untilled wastes; or again by marrying, like Shakespeare's father, into the gentry; or merely by staying put for generations and gaining the respect of neighbours. Jeremiads about the 'decay' of the yeomanry are a frequent theme of this and many other generations; they are true only of a much later age. Whatever losses the yeomanry may have suffered to the gentry were amply compensated by recruitment to their own ranks from below; there is abundant evidence that the grade was a numerous and flourishing one. Latimer maintained that yeomen were the backbone of the Reformation: 'By yeomen's sons the faith of Christ is and hath been maintained chiefly', he declared in one of his sermons. But then Latimer was a yeoman's son himself!

Then there was the tenant farmer, hardly distinguishable from the yeoman save in the legal drawback that his tenure was more precarious. Old and substantial tenants of an estate were for practical purposes as safe as freeholders. It was a matter of pride to keep the same body of tenants on one's estate from father to son, generation after generation. True, it was no longer legal to have them wearing your livery or fighting your private wars (though both were still known to happen where the law was weak), but the same spirit would impel you to marshal them behind you at election time, even if the election was uncontested. It was worth a little patience over rents in bad times, as every wise steward knew, to retain this tie. For the pride was reciprocal: on old-fashioned estates the landlord was still a lord of men as well as of land, and the tenantry instinctively rallied to him in time of crisis. Even if the obligation to vote at elections for the landlord or his nominee was not a condition of tenure, as in some Elizabethan leases, the idea of doing anything else would hardly have occurred to his dependants before political divisions began to cut across older loyalties in the next century.

And not elections only: many of the disorders that still spasmodically troubled town life were due to the flocking in of a litigant's *clientèle* to back up their patron's feuds in the courts. The streets of Shrewsbury at the spring assizes of the Armada year were thronged with 'sutche a boundance of people, that the lycke hath not been seene', because two Montgomeryshire litigants—Edward Herbert of Montgomery castle and Owen Vaughan of Llwydiarth, who were at perpetual feud with each other—had each brought his following to the town; in the following January Herbert's son-in-law, a Shrewsbury man, stirred things up again by sending his trumpeter to challenge the hostile contingent, who wisely avoided a 'bloody day' (but for 'half-a-dozen broken pates') by staying indoors. Such scenes were far from uncommon.

Copyholders were by now a legal

A peasant tilling

category only. The status of villeinage had ceased to exist in England—not through any statute of manumission, but through enlightened legal practice, by virtue of which the copyholder who could display in the queen's court the 'copy of court roll' certifying the conditions on which he or his villein forbears had held their land was as secure in his tenure, so long as those conditions were fulfilled, as the freeholder. The villein's son or grandson might now be as well-to-do as the freeman's; many copy-

A copyholder's house

holders had raised themselves to yeoman status, and it was even whispered that a close scrutiny would reveal the taint of villeinage in the ancestry of not a few of the gentry themselves, perhaps even of esquires or knights. Yet on the whole the copyholder tended to find his level among the smallholders and cottagers, and there still hung about him—now and for centuries to come, as readers of Thomas Hardy's story 'Netty Sargent's copyhold' will recall—a certain aura of insecurity, as well as the slight stigma attaching to exclusion from the franchise. The copyholder for life could never be sure his children would inherit; even the copyholder by inheritance had to face an uncertain fine at each demise. For this reason leasehold was considered a safer tenure. On many crown lordships in Wales Queen Elizabeth made a composition with her copyholders under which they surrendered their copyholds in return for the grant of long leases. The transaction involved a fine, which might range from £10 to over £200, and often had to be borrowed; but the general effect was to give an established— often a highly respected—position in society to descendants of the old bond tenants, the nearest equivalent in Welsh law to the English villein.

Far more precarious was the position of the tenant-at-will and the landless labourer. This last class is another which the social disruptions of the dying middle ages had tended to multiply. The ploughman, cowman and other permanent residential farm servants on a yearly wage had been familiar

Farm servants: shepherd and cowherd

figures in rural society since the first emergence of a free labouring class; the day labourer was a newer phenomenon. In Elizabethan wage assessments he normally takes pride of place, whereas earlier Statutes of Labourers do not recognise his existence. Yet farm labour had not yet become the general sump of the unskilled. Elizabeth's Statute of Artificers still includes it among the skilled crafts to which apprenticeship is the proper entry. And for many of these yokels the word 'landless' is an overstatement, for, as Hales puts it, they were often able to supplement what they got by their 'handie labours' by 'some refreshinge upon the . . . commons'—if it were only the right to gather firewood or turf, a goose-run or woodland 'pannage' for a pig—unless enclosure had robbed them of it. Indeed, if an Elizabethan law of 1589 had remained more than a pious aspiration, no labourer would have had less than four acres of land attached to his cottage.

The so-called Tudor enclosure 'movement', which called forth the diatribes of More, Latimer and the rest, was simply an intensification, for limited ends, in limited areas and for a limited period, of what had long been, and long remained, a normal process of the countryside. By Elizabeth's time its force was already spent, although laws against depopulation, unheeded because unenforceable, kept cropping up on the statute book almost to the end of her reign. But if the spectacular conversion of arable to pasture was abating because it no longer paid the same dividends, the normal processes of 'colonisation'—draining

Fishing

26

of fenland, clearing of forest, and ordinary intakes from the waste—went steadily ahead; so too did that other form of enclosure, the consolidation, by agreement, by legal process or by various forms of sharp

Sheep farming

practice, of arable strips in the 'town lands'; and so far from encountering, even on paper, the legal obstacles put in the way of turning 'houses of husbandry' into sheep farms, this process was positively encouraged by an Act of 1597. The classes most liable to suffer from all this were naturally those with the most precarious tenures: copyholders for life, tenants at will, cottagers accustomed to some 'refreshing' on the commons; and contemporary Jeremiahs were loud in their denunciation of the 'insatiable cormorants' who dispossessed them, causing so many village riots and lawsuits. The blame was generally laid at the door of successful merchants stepping out of their class to buy up manors and lordships and treating them as business investments as well as avenues to gentility.

Examples of these are not hard to find. In 1595 Thomas Myddelton invested nearly £5,000 of the proceeds of his export trade and his Spanish booty in the purchase of a crown lordship in Wales, partly with a view to reclaiming on behalf of his 'lyttle son' the position his remote ancestors had once held in Welsh society, but partly for more material reasons: the five manors of the lordship were estimated to bring in £150 a year in rents, but he notes in his ledger that 'by the opinion of moste men' this could easily be raised to £250. Within two years of the purchase he is up before Star Chamber on charges of unlawful enclosure. It was incidents like this that impressed contemporaries: less notice was taken of the quiet but steady encroachments of the yeoman (perhaps the biggest encloser of them all) or the inching of the cottager into the adjacent waste by the sweat of his brow.

27

Yet with it all there was little change in the fundamental pattern of the countryside. Forests were receding, but enough remained to leave the stag hunt still the king of sports; in the woodlands of the south-west the fallow-deer ran wild, and in Wales and Cumberland even the wolf was not extinct. Marshland was being drained piecemeal, but in the undrained Fens, stretching for nearly seventy miles through the shires or

'Champion' country: open fields at Laxton, Nottinghamshire

Cambridge, Huntingdon and Lincoln, a race of men apart (of 'brutish unciviliz'd tempers' according to Camden) went on stilts about their business of grazing, fishing and fowling, like French shepherds of the Landes. In widely scattered parts of the country the familiar quickset hedge had made its appearance as a result of old or new enclosures, the former notably in Kent, the latter in the south midlands; but most of England was still 'champion' or open country—open enough for Rupert's cavalry to gallop freely over it in the next century—where the ploughland lay in intermingled strips diversified only by compacter blocks here and there where strips had been exchanged or engrossed by purchase.

In such conditions there was not much scope for change in methods of tillage. The cumbrous medieval

Haymaking

wooden plough, now more generously shod with iron, was still in general use, and the ox was widely preferred to the horse for drawing it. With few exceptions, the most notable being the introduction of hops earlier in the century, the same crops were grown in the familiar traditional rotation; and the routine of the farmer's year, hinging on the church's saints' days and festivals, was unaffected by the religious revolution. The prevailing cereal crop naturally varied with the character of the soil, but rye, the general basis of the loaf save for the more prosperous classes, was the most universal. Root crops were confined to the kitchen garden. The biggest changes were to be seen in those areas which were learning to concentrate on producing beef, corn or fruit to meet the ever-growing demands of the London market: the home counties, East Anglia and the southern midlands; and the environs of other large towns, in their varying degrees, were feeling the same impetus. A few counties were gaining a reputation for local specialities like Cheshire and Suffolk cheeses, which gave them a market beyond their own bounds; in others the yield of the soil was being improved by marling, liming and manuring, and attention to animal husbandry was producing a better weight of meat. The reign saw a brisk output of practical books on farming—a new vogue in literature, and a popular one: Tusser, writing in homespun verse, went into a dozen or more editions before the queen died. Precepts couched in this form, and based on experience rather than on theory, were apt to be listened to; at any rate the middle years of the reign were on the whole a good time for agriculture when the annual rental on some estates (it has been reckoned) 'climbed to a third of what those estates had sold for a decade earlier'.

Yet there was no agrarian revolution; how could there be, when biology and chemistry were still in their medieval swaddling-bands and when custom, enforced in the court leet, reigned supreme wherever 'champion farming' and manorial economy prevailed, which meant over most of England? A gentleman who looked for a better return from his land saw the quickest way in enclosure and rack-renting or in marrying into more and better land; if this failed, then he would more likely invest his capital in the reversion to a profitable job, or more cheaply still in the hopeful gift of a butt of sack to a prominent courtier and spices for his lady, than in any expensive improvements in soil or stock.

For landlord and peasant alike rural industry provided some diversity in rural life and often a supplement to their returns from the land itself. Apart from the more ubiquitous and time-less village crafts, the Elizabethan age (as will appear more fully in another context) was remarkable for the extension, in suitable areas of the countryside, of industries serving more than local needs, such as mining, smelting and woollens. With the exception of a few developed industries like the Tyneside collieries, mining tended to be part of the normal working of the estate under which the coal or ores lay, with the labourers employed seasonally in mine or field under the steward's direction; or else it was an enterprise undertaken singly or in groups by working miners under immemorial custom or licence from the crown, as with Cornish tin, the lead of Somerset, Derby and Flint or the coal and ironstone of the Forest of Dean. But everywhere Elizabethan land-lords were tending to encroach on these ancient privileges. The pure industrial capitalist, inter-vening between the owner of minerals and those who actually

A village blacksmith at work

30

worked them, was as novel and exceptional outside well-established mining areas as the full-time miner divorced from the land. Similarly smelting was largely a rural industry; depending as it did in the main on charcoal, not 'sea-coal', it was widely dispersed through the woodland shires, with points of concentration in the Sussex Weald and the Forest of Dean; and it carried in its wake another ancient country craft, that of charcoal-burner.

Spinning and carding

In the cloth industry the novelty, though one that went back well beyond Elizabeth's reign, was the migration of skilled workers to country districts, where home weaving and spinning had always been widely practised by the peasant and his family on an evening or when field-work was slack. Only in advanced clothing districts like East Anglia, the West Riding or the south-west would textile work be a specialised occupation unmixed with agriculture; and here the employer was not the landlord but the merchant clothier in the neighbouring 'clothing' town: Norwich or York, Exeter or Bristol. But even outside these areas the part-time peasant weaver was often glad to sacrifice independence for a steady market by becoming a virtual out-worker to some urban merchant company near at hand. In this way the widespread cottage industry of North Wales fell in Elizabethan days under the control first of middlemen from Oswestry and then of the far more powerful Drapers' Company of Shrewsbury, where the skilled finishing processes were performed; but for long after this the local industry retained its primitive peasant character.

This brings us to those two 'under-developed' regions, Wales and the North, both of them living under a pastoral economy with a little subsistence farming, both honeycombed with survivals of an earlier order: military feudalism in the North, Celtic tribalism in Wales. But here the resemblance ends. The North 'knew no other Prince than a Percy', and the Percys looked to the past; the assimilation of the North was not achieved until after a final revolt in 1569, and the new social order did not finally emerge there before the next reign. Wales, on the other hand, developed a new loyalty to a line of kings of her own race, helped to the throne by the arms of her own soldiers and the more peaceful propaganda of her bards. And so out of the wreckage of tribal society, begun long ago under her own native princes and now completed by Tudor policy, came a new breed of Welsh gentry ready to exercise their ancestral leadership (for few of them were really 'new men') within the new administrative machine; ready also to take advantage of all the opportunities it offered for building up their individual estates and establishing their families unhampered by the periodic subdivision of lands which Welsh law had imposed. Geography and royal favour gave them a pull over the northerners in easier access to court and capital. By Elizabeth's day they had dug themselves in, combining authority under the crown and the 'port' of an English gentle-man—often a severe strain on their more meagre resources—with an instinctive appeal at home to ancient loyalties with their concomitant feuds, and the common inheritance and guardian-ship of an ancient culture.

The complex task of fitting the other classes of Welsh tribal society to the procrustean bed of English law was a long-drawn headache, but a very profitable one, to the lawyers. The process of English conquest had left much of Wales crown land, and it was on these lands that the pattern of the new society was chiefly worked out; that it was completed without violent up-heaval, though by no means without ruinous litigation, is

Weaving

perhaps a tribute to the rough justice done. Elizabethan Wales emerged as a society without a titled aristocracy, but pivoted on a wide-ranging class of gentry which modelled itself on that of England; the younger sons disinherited by the new law of primogeniture drifted into commerce and the professions or into the lower ranks of rural society in company with the former bond tenants and the less fortunate of the free tribesmen. And the face of the countryside remained essentially unchanged.

Further Reading

M. Campbell *The English Yeoman*, 1944.

Ernle, *English Farming, Past and Present*, 1912.

Hasbach, *A History of the English Agricultural Labourer* (trans. R. Kenyon), 1920.

J. U. Nef, *The Rise of the British Coal Industry*, Vol. I (illustrated), 1932.

J. Rhys and D. Brynmor-Jones, *The Welsh People*, 1900.

R. H. Tawney, *The Agrarian Problem in the Sixteenth Century*, 1912.

H. R. Trevor-Roper, 'The Gentry, 1541–1640', *Economic History Review Supplement*.

III

Town Life

It is usually reckoned that not more than a fifth of the inhabitants of Elizabethan England were townsmen, and even the townsman, as we shall see, was nine times out of ten a countryman at heart, in close touch with country life and dreaming of the day when he might retire there for good. Yet the influence of towns was out of all proportion to their size and population; nearly all of them were rapidly increasing in size and, still more important, in wealth. Head and shoulders above them all towered London, at least ten times as populous as any other English town, bigger than any other in northern Europe, defying all attempts to check its growth, and already such a force in politics as to be something like a fourth estate of the realm. Estimates of its population during the reign vary from one to three hundred thousand. Much depends on whether one looks at the beginning or the end of the reign, during which it may easily have doubled itself; much on what is included of the swelling population outside the walls, to say nothing of the city of Westminster, or of the inhabitants of town houses occupied only when parliament and law courts were sitting or when the royal court was in residence.

The city of London proper, still girt with its full complement of walls and gates, was becoming more and more the domain of merchants living and doing business in those vast houses so many of which fell victims to the Great Fire a century later, conducting their civic affairs at Guildhall, administering their various 'trades' in the lavish halls of the twelve city companies and worshipping in the city's hundred and more churches, of which only five survive today; concluding business deals

The Lord Mayor of London

there often enough too, until Elizabeth's Royal Exchange provided more seemly quarters. The wealthier of them—and some were fabulously wealthy—had more commodious mansions outside the walls, or even country houses in Surrey or Essex. The aristocracy who formerly had their houses in the city itself were also rapidly moving out to lordly palaces along the extra-mural waterfront and the Strand. The dissolution of the monasteries marked an important stage in this process, for the westward and north-westward expansion of London had been blocked by great monastic properties. Those of the Templars, secularised since the fourteenth century, had become the legal quarter of London, the home of the Inns of Court. When Henry VIII completed the job, a teeming population drifted into the vacuum, spreading past the hamlet of Charing towards the city of Westminster, where the two royal palaces of Whitehall and Westminster attracted another human swarm concerned with the work of government.

Yet the country was never far away. John Stow the tailor, a Londoner *pur sang* if ever there was one, remembered in his old age, towards the close of the queen's reign, how as a lad in her grandfather's day he had many a time trudged for the milk from his Cornhill home, where a quintain used to be set up for 'merry disports' at Christmastide, to a farm near Aldgate with a herd of thirty or forty milch kine; here he would buy for a halfpenny three pints in summer and a quart in winter, 'always hot from the kine'. When he wrote his immortal

35

Survey of London this country lane had been largely built over, but there were plenty of other fields and open spaces. The built-up area extended only from a mile to half-a-mile north of the river; east of the Tower it was narrower still, consisting of a 'filthy strait passage, with alleys . . . inhabited by sailors' victuallers' (and by seamen themselves), sprawling for a mile or so along Thames-side towards Wapping and Limehouse. These too were largely on old monastic or episcopal manors. Stow was much perturbed at the recent encroachment of 'cottages and alleys' on Whitechapel's green common, spoiling a pleasant approach to the city. But northwards there still lay vast open spaces where the citizenry had their 'mayings', where the trainbands could exercise, and where the first theatres were built. Across London Bridge, with its fine array of shops and houses, was the outlying borough of Southwark, another area where houses were rapidly encroaching on monastic lands, and another centre for recreation; for here stood the bear garden and the later Bankside theatres. Not surprisingly, it had an unsavoury reputation as a haunt of outlaws, cut-

City, London Bridge and the Tower

purses and prostitutes—a metaphorical as well as a literal bear-garden.

If you wanted to cross the river at any other point (to the primate's palace at Lambeth, say), you had perforce to resort to the knavish wherrymen, whom you might also use, if you could afford it, as your taximen from point to point in London proper. For the Thames was still London's main highway, although Stow complains that ancient regulations limiting the use of wheeled vehicles in the city's narrow streets are falling into abeyance; London already had its traffic problems. On the remoter periphery, but within easy reach, were country villages like Chelsea or Paddington, St. Pancras, St. Giles or Islington; the queen used to hunt at Marylebone, and on Bethnal Green they said the fairies still danced.

What gave London its standing as a fourth estate, however, was the influence it exercised far and wide over the realm at large. This radiated from four main quarters. First from Westminster: outwards through the judges on circuit, the officials and poursuivants carrying the orders of the court to the

London Bridge in 1578

four corners of the land; inwards through the incursion every few years of the parliament men from shires and boroughs. For the weeks or months of the session's duration they would find lodgings in the city and come under the lure of its playhouses and other delights, and then return to appease their womenfolk by the gift of a gown or a gown-length from Cheapside—one of the many ways in which London fashions spread through the countryside. The wealthier would take family and servants with them to their own town houses, or perhaps borrow or rent one of these fine houses on the Strand, but the habit did not spread to the rank and file of members until sessions grew longer; till then they were content to do the journey on horseback with such retinue as they could muster or hire, and to return as soon as they could.

Next the legal quarter; not only did the country gentry often carry their endless legal quarrels to the courts at Westminster, but they also sent their sons to one of the Inns of Court after

The Royal Exchange, built in 1566 and opened by the Queen in 1571

The Thames as London's highway: Billingsgate in 1598

(or even instead of) Oxford or Cambridge. For by Elizabeth's
time these had become 'finishing schools' for laymen as well
as professional schools for lawyers; the student carried home
with him something even more important than London fashions:
a smattering of politics and law—perhaps even a critical attitude
towards government, ominous for the next reign. The third
influence, that of London's incipient theatreland, can best be
treated in another context, but the commercial and financial
sway of the city proper was one of the decisive factors in national
life.

Frequent and bitter were contemporary complaints of how the
wealthy London exporter, by his weight of capital and his
access to foreign markets, was engrossing the trade of the

Country meets town: Eastcheap market in 1598

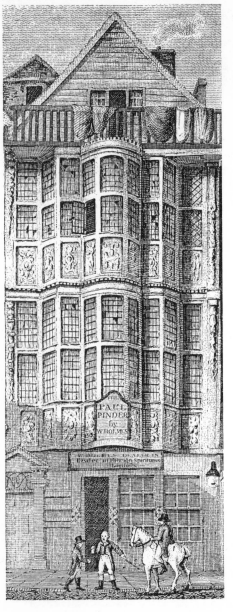

The house of a wealthy London merchant

provincial towns, compelling, for example, the Norwich or Shrewsbury draper to bring his cloth for sale abroad to the depôt at Blackwell Hall, and so controlling both prices and, in the long run, employment; of how the London importer, by encouraging the new taste for foreign luxuries, was undermining well-established local crafts like those of the Chester capper, the Bristol lace-maker, or the threadmaker of Coventry. Then too there were those regional or nation-wide monopolies, like Ralegh's in Cornish tin, which the queen granted to favoured courtiers or to new joint-stock companies financed from London: a familiar instance is the Company for the Mines Royal, which opened up new copper and lead mines in Cumberland, Wales and Cornwall in the interest of the munition supplies of a nation at war. These also brought their quota of provincial grumbles, now against the greedy metropolis and the insatiable courtiers, now against the skilled foreigners imported to direct the work. The moneylender, commonly a merchant who had prospered and turned financier, had an even wider sway, for country squires as well as provincial dealers often fell into his clutches. The machinery of credit had not kept pace with the expansion of trade, and legal limits to the rate of interest proved hard to enforce; Thomas Myddelton, who was no extortioner, always expected and got his ten per cent, and his debtors ranged from noblemen, admirals, colonels and statesmen down to country clothiers, parsons and landlords—especially the poor but aspiring gentry of his native Wales.

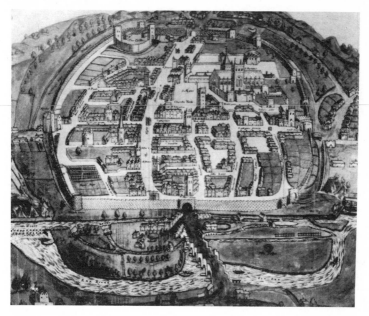

Exeter, a flourishing seaport, in 1587

Yet all the evidence goes to show that, at least until the economic crisis brought about by prolonged war towards the end of the reign, most of the provincial towns were thriving too. Norwich, the chief seat of the textile industry; Bristol, the second port, but with customs only a twentieth those of London; York the capital of the North—each of them with some ten to twenty thousand inhabitants; then below them a larger group with

Bakers of York. From the Ordinances
of their Guild, 1595–96

about five thousand apiece. Most of these were ruled by narrow merchant oligarchies, less wealthy, of course, than the city fathers of London, but still well-to-do in comparison with their country neighbours. Exeter, a flourishing seaport, probably stood about midway between this grade of town and the ten thousand class; here a very small group had accumulated fortunes running into five figures, and the lower limit of income for substantial merchants has been reckoned at about £100, whereas the estates of the smaller surrounding gentry ranged between £50 and £100. But the merchant's fortune was more precarious than the gentleman's. Much of it was locked up in bad debts, and the defaulting customer was more slippery to handle than the defaulting tenant. Besides, the uncertainties of foreign trade could throw even a flourishing shipper into the clutches of the 'usurer'; *The Merchant of Venice* was written for a public only too familiar with Antonio's predicament.

What is noticeable everywhere is the tendency of municipal government to fall into the hands of an ever-narrowing merchant clique, leaving outside the citadel of power those who were primarily concerned with the making of goods. These wholesalers generally controlled the incorporated companies of the various trades and crafts, pale replicas of those of London, and successors to the medieval craft gilds, but now too exclusive to cater for the working craftsman himself. Exeter had eight such companies at the opening of the reign, and during its course four more were added, bringing the total up to London's own; smaller towns had to make do with one or two. Not infrequently a single company like the drapers of Shrewsbury, Coventry or Worcester, or in seaport towns like Bristol or Exeter or even an inland market like York a civic company of Merchant Adventurers, was able to control the entire trade of a town, though never without an outcry from the retailers against monopoly.

The control exercised by these local oligarchs covered every side of the townsman's life. First and foremost trade: the enforcement of apprenticeship, the regulation of markets, standards and prices, the exclusion of 'foreigners' (which of course might mean the man from the next town as well as the alien), the settlement of the frequent 'demarcation' disputes between trades which so often transport one into the atmosphere of the modern trade union world. And 'foreigners' included the hordes of vagrants against whom the town felt it necessary to take strong measures *pour encourager les autres*, without too nice a discrimination between the genuine unemployed and the habitual tramp: the unsuccessful had short shrift in Elizabethan England. On the other hand, for their own genuine poor most towns made reasonably humane provision, whether by charitable benefaction or through compulsory rates, as provided by the many Elizabethan Poor Laws. Of this, and of municipal provision for education, more will be said later on.

A wealthy townsman and his wife

Then there was the moral as well as the material welfare of the townsman to be looked after. The apprentice must not be allowed to strut about in the fine feathers appropriate to the man who

43

has succeeded in life, as an Exeter boy found when he was fined for celebrating the Christmas of 1561 in ruffs and a silken hat. As for the 'spiv', the same city provides an example of a gambler who had tempted grammar school boys into debts they could meet only by pawning their school books; he had to disgorge his winnings and to redeem the books—what happened to the boys is not on record. All town authorities were much preoccupied with drunkenness and the regulation of alehouses; they could not afford to shut their eyes even to the milder offences of bickering and backbiting, which were just as liable to lead to breaches of the peace, and the ducking stool was always at hand to quell the common scold. Witch hunts were more often of the nature of lynch law. Many of the more crowded towns were now setting night watches to see that burgesses kept decent hours and that strangers did not intrude by stealth. In the absence of chiming clocks, still rare outside London, they were also useful in singing out the hours:

> *Twelve o'clock, look well to your locks,*
> *Your fire and your light, and so good night.*

Street lighting was left to the private householder, and precautions against fire were miserably inadequate to the danger in those generously timbered Elizabethan houses. Leading townsmen were expected to keep leather buckets handy in case of an outbreak, but the authorities were, significantly, more concerned with providing implements for demolishing houses to which it might spread. We have all learned from Dogberry and Verges to take a poor view of Elizabethan police arrangements, but not all constables can have been Dogberrys, or trade would have come to a standstill. Merchants often had thousands of pounds' worth of jewels and other stuff lying in their warehouses unscathed; but of course most of these hired a private 'watch'.

The bellman

Health came a poor second to morals and the maintenance of public order—

44

A water-carrier

except when plague was raging or imminent, and something had to be done urgently to keep it in bounds. Then perhaps the civic authorities would stir themselves to enforce preventive regulations long on their order books 'to see the streets made clean every day saving Sunday' (the duty of the private householder except where, as at Manchester, hired men were taken on to sweep out the all-important markets), 'to warn inhabitants to keep channels against their houses free from filth', or not to make 'dung-hills out of stables . . . in the street'; but when the plague subsided these excellent intentions were apt to be forgotten again. Pure water was a commodity almost unknown outside country towns or villages lucky enough to have a river or wells which had not yet become a general receptacle for sewage. The year after the Armada the Fleet river was cleansed and scoured from springs at Hampstead so that London 'should be served of fresh water in all places of want'; but the £600 or £700 it cost the rate-payers were largely thrown away, for before the end of the reign, Stow tells us, the Fleet, thanks to encroachment on the banks and 'casting of soilage into the stream', had become 'worse cloyed and choken than ever it was before'. Many a provincial town council and even rural court leet could have told the same tale in miniature right down to the nineteenth century. The Londoner was luckier than most townsmen in that at least some parts of the city were served with water by leaden conduits (useful for quenching fires also) which had been erected at public or private expense at various times since the thirteenth century, and an 'engine' was erected for pumping it in 1594; but even London had to wait for anything approaching an adequate water supply till Thomas Myddelton's brother Hugh undertook the construction of the New River in the next reign.

On the other hand we must not think of a Tudor town in terms of modern urban congestion. Towns such as those men-tioned above held a population of a fifth, a tenth or even a twentieth that of today in an area not conspicuously smaller, so there was still plenty of elbow-room, plenty of gardens, orchards and pleasant riverside walks—and no smoke to speak of. The air was clean if the water was not. However rapid the drift to the towns, it could be accommodated without building back-to-back houses or noisome slum tenements. Cottages were not as a rule built in rows, but individually, each with its own 'backside' in which vegetables and herbs could be grown and a pig kept: at least the absence of such amenities was novel enough to call for comment. And if there was no conscious town-planning and only the sketchiest of building lines—for encroachment of houses, shops and pigstyes on highways and footwalks was a constant worry to the town authorities—carpenters and master masons had their pride (fostered by the gild) and their distinctive skills (passed on by apprenticeship) to ensure in architectural pattern and in general lay-out the maintenance of traditional standards without standardisation. Nor must we forget, on the subject of the health of towns, that there were towns already recognised as health resorts. Lord Burghley often took his gout away to Buxton for a cure; on a lower plane Thomas Myddelton sent his ailing younger brother twice to Bath by horse-litter.

It would be a mistake to imagine any country town, however remote, as completely out of reach of medical help. Sometimes a fully qualified doctor, with an Oxford or even a Padua degree, would settle in his home town and practise there, usually with some other occupation to eke out his fees, and then the succession would be kept up by apprenticeship. Naturally he would depend mainly on the custom of the surrounding gentry, for his fees must needs be high—so high that even the government boggled at an S.O.S. for more doctors from plague-stricken English forces serving abroad in 1563, on the ground that medical men 'required greater entertainment than was allowed'. When Myddelton's brother came home to Denbigh to die, three doctors' visits cost the London merchant as much as £13 10s.—far more than the traditional 13s. 4d. a visit. No doubt fees were adjusted to the length of the patient's purse. But about a dozen years later this enterprising little borough embarked on what might almost be called a municipal medical service: it admitted as burgess, without fee, a surgeon who had been apprenticed to another local doctor (Myddelton's perhaps), on condition that he would 'at all times . . . heale and cure every burges dwelling in the said town . . ., taking such wages for every the said cures as the Aldermen, Bayliffes and Capitall Burgesses . . . shall award'. We can hardly call

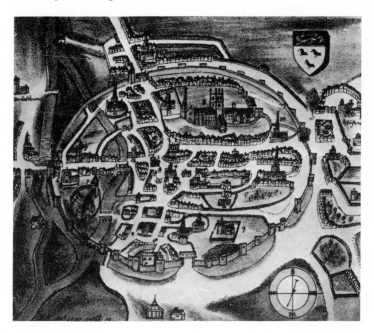

Canterbury in 1588

him a medical officer to the town, for there is no sign that he had any responsibility for the town drains (if any), and the burgesses—a select body—would all be men of means. There was no doubt substance in Bishop Latimer's complaint that 'at our time, physic is a remedy only for rich folks, . . . for the poor is not able to wage the physician'. Unless, as sometimes happened, the local parson had some stock prescriptions tucked away with his sermon notes and passed them on gratis to the poor parishioners, these must needs make the best they could of

47

family nostrums and 'simples' from the garden, or else submit themselves to the tender mercies of the barber surgeon or the 'wise woman'.

Much has been said above—much was said by contemporaries —about the exclusiveness of Tudor towns: not only their frosty reception of the penniless vagrant, but their jealousy of even the skilled 'foreigner' seeking a job. 'Wheare other cities doe alure unto them goode workemen', declares the Doctor in Hales's *Discourse of the Common Weal*, 'oure men will expell theim oute.' Yet the majority of mayors of Exeter in the latter half of the century were either newcomers or sons of newcomers, generally from the surrounding country, but many from farther afield. Most of the larger English boroughs had their Dick Whittingtons. If the rich merchant controlled the crafts, as he in turn was so often dominated by the London exporter, the enter- prising craftsman could get his own back by becoming a merchant. The country might grumble at the town but it was glad to send its children, even children of gentry, to be apprenticed there. The country gentleman himself, if things were going badly on the land, was not above seeking his fortune in trade in the town. Many 'county' people were fain to seek a borough seat in parliament when the county seat was booked. The smaller, weaker boroughs welcomed the chance of shifting the expense on to the shoulders of one whose 'quality' would make him a far more effective advocate in parliament when borough interests were at stake. Even the more imposing boroughs, for all their show of independence, did not disdain the patronage of a local magnate who might keep their end up at the court itself. Besides, if the country lad came to town, many a townsman's dream was to retire on his gains to the land, or as one of them

Market women

acidly put it, to 'creep and seek to be a gentleman'. Thus 'the city', it has been said of Exeter, 'was a kind of neutral ground where scions of the gentry, the yeomanry, and of husbandmen met on equal terms to contend for the prize

48

of economic success and the rewards of social prestige which followed it'.

Interior of a shop

We can go farther than this, and say that the line between country and town was often as tenuous as that between gentleman and yeoman. All but the more populous towns were still bordered by their town fields. To these many a townsman would trudge out day by day to labour like his country cousins. The Elizabethan country town (and a very few Elizabethan towns were not in this category) like Thomas Hardy's Dorchester 'lived by agriculture at one remove further from the fountain-head than the adjoining villages—no more'. What distinguished the small town from the large village was often simply whatever measure of self-government its charter conferred, and especially the right to own corporate property. This the townsman valued highly when it was a question of keeping at bay the sheriff, the deputy lieutenant and the county magistrates in matters like the assessment of taxes and the mustering of the militia; he was less enthusiastic when it saddled him with costly duties like the upkeep, repair or rebuilding of a town bridge which the county used as well. For six years from 1575 to 1581, the tiny borough, as it then was, of Cardiff fought the county over the rebuilding of its collapsed bridge, for which borough funds were miserably inadequate; and by playing on the inevitable county feuds the town had its way.

In the small country town the place of the merchant oligarch of Bristol, Norwich or York was taken by the thriving shopkeeper, selling his own wares in his own house, together with the professional man of good standing, all of them generally sons or dependants of the local gentry. The country doctor has been touched upon; the country parson will concern us later. Most influential of all, perhaps, was the country lawyer. In Elizabethan England he made a good income and lived in style. Few towns, however small, could dispense with his services in the innumerable trading disputes and contested claims to land that were bound to arise in an age when manorial economy was in decay, land rapidly changing hands and old trade barriers breaking down. But a borough might even have no wealthy class at all, and stand in as complete dependence on the country gentry as any other village. For the grant of a charter was very much a matter of historical chance. Edward I's military boroughs in North Wales were often little more than annexes to the castle for the accommodation of the butcher and baker and candlestick-maker serving the civil needs of the garrison; and when the garrison was no more needed they sank back into villages—but kept their charters. Elsewhere trade had taken a new direction and left a once flourishing borough high and dry; or else the sea had encroached and left most of it under the waves or the sand dunes—but still a borough.

Conversely there were unincorporated villages now developing into centres of industry and population and struggling with the problems of the Elizabethan industrial revolution on the very inadequate machinery of the court leet. Manchester, an ancient market town which had never fully developed into a 'free' borough, was rapidly gaining a name for its local speciality of rough woollens, important enough by 1580 to find their way to the continent through the port of Chester, which tried to monopolise the trade. The industry was organised under 'clothiers' employing a substantial number of domestic weavers, and

Elizabeth's charter to Beaumaris, 1561

often leaving large fortunes. One of them, Anthony Mosley, pushed the family sales, in defiance of Chester, in the London market itself, to the point of becoming lord mayor there and purchasing the manor of Manchester. But the town remained under the government of its manorial court leet—village machinery trying desperately to cope with urban problems, especially of sanitation and recurrent plague; nearly three hundred years were to pass before it received its charter. Meanwhile, as one of Manchester's historians picturesquely puts it, 'pigs still snuffled hungrily among the garbage in its main streets, and new barns were still being built in Deansgate'.

Much the same could be said of Sheffield, Birmingham or Leeds. Sheffield was the centre of a wide rural area largely employed in making first scythes, then 'whittles' (popularly worn in place of swords by those who were not quite gentlemen) and finally domestic cutlery which was winning a nation-wide repute. Yet Sheffield remained, cutlers and all, under the complete domination of the earl of Shrewsbury as lord of the manor. Camden found Birmingham ('Bremicham' to him) 'swarming with inhabitants, and echoing with the noise of anvils', with 'abundance of handsome buildings' in the upper part of the town; but Birmingham too was under its manorial lord, though he held the reins loosely enough to leave the Birmingham metal workers probably the most independent body of artisans, for better or for worse, in the whole of England. Leeds had been described in Henry VII's reign as 'a pretty market town, standing by its clothing'; between the reigns of Edward VI and Elizabeth its sales of this 'clothing' increased tenfold, but it received no borough charter till the time of Charles I. The Elizabethan 'new towns' were in the main old and hitherto stagnant urban centres now sprouting into new life, not mushroom growths springing out of nothing, like the worst horrors of the early machine age. The continuity of town life, as of country life, was unbroken.

Further Reading

CONTEMPORARY

J. Stow, *Survey of London*, 1603 (ed. Wheatley, Everyman's Library).

LATER

W. T. MacCaffrey, *Exeter, 1540–1640*, 1958.

A. Redford, *History of Local Government in Manchester*, Vol. I, 1939.

G. Unwin, *Industrial Organization in the Sixteenth and Seventeenth Centuries*, 1904.

IV

Home Life

The increasing luxury of the Elizabethan age is proverbial. Moralists lashed it, satirists laughed at it, patriots vaunted it, writers on housewifery enjoined it, dramatists depicted it, and household account books have survived in plenty to attest it. It was a natural consequence of the general prosperity and the great expansion of our commerce in foreign luxuries that marked the second half of the century. It affected all classes except the lowest grade of unskilled labourer, 'the poor', the most unchanging class of society not only in that they are always with us, but because change begins with luxuries, and luxuries seldom come their way.

The most obvious effect is seen in the houses themselves. At the top of the scale come such palatial extravagances as Theobalds in Hertfordshire, Longleat in Wiltshire or Hardwick in Derbyshire. The queen, with a dozen palaces to choose from, felt no urgent desire to add to them: building was not among her interests or her extravagances. It was left to wealthy subjects to rehouse themselves on a princely scale; and the houses they built bear all the marks of the superb confidence, the omnivorous curiosity, the unbridled exuberance of the age, with more than a touch of the ostentatious vulgarity of the *nouveau riche*. It is perhaps significant that the three houses just mentioned were all built by men or women who had risen rapidly to fortune from the ranks of the middling country gentry. Burghley is the clearest case in point. He sprang from an ancient but undistinguished line of Welsh border squires; his immediate forbears had taken full advantage of the opportunities Tudor England offered to their kind, and they left him 'Burleigh-house by Stamford-town', built on monastic property at the dissolution. He began at once to enlarge it, and the process was completed, on a scale of growing magnificence to match his rising fortunes, just before the Armada sailed. The plans were his own, based on careful study of French and Flemish models. Meanwhile his public duties called for a London residence, and he satisfied this need by buying a half-finished house in Covent Garden; this cost him some £2,000, and even before it was finished he was able to entertain the

Longleat House, Wiltshire, 1547–80

queen there. But his chief care was lavished on Theobalds, built on a Hertfordshire manor which he bought as an estate for his infant son. The existing moated manor house was found inadequate when the queen visited him there in 1564, and in the next ten years he set about building in its stead, again from his own foreign-inspired plans, a palace fit for a queen, which indeed became the favourite palace of a king when Burghley's son surrendered it to James I and built Hatfield instead. What Theobalds cost Burghley we do not know, but at the peak of building his yearly expenses on it ran to nearly £3,000; yet scarce a stone remains of it today.

The builders of Hardwick and Longleat both grew from the same sort of roots: 'Bess of Hardwick', with an unimpressive ancestry of Derbyshire gentry, owed her fortune to a superb business head which enabled her to get the better of everyone she dealt with, including four successive husbands; Sir John Thynne, who came of minor Shropshire stock, won his way in the well-paid service of Protector Somerset. There were few others who could build on this scale; maybe it was just as well, for there is a beauty quieter, perhaps more harmonious, certainly more redolent of the soil, in the reconstructed country manor houses of the age. Here the builder had to reduce the architectural novelties of the great house to a more modest compass, and could bring in foreign fashions only to the extent of employing masons who had encountered them, at third or fourth remove, on English soil. The great house stood for the revolutionary aspect of the age; the small country house for its continuity with the English past. Yet the new type of house, great or small, made a great impression on contemporaries. Harrison tells us that what chiefly struck old men in his village, apart from the growing comfort and seemliness of internal domestic arrangements, was the 'multitude of chimneys lately erected, whereas in their young days there were not above two or three, if so many, in most uplandish towns of the realm'.

A northern manor-house: Ince Hall, near Wigan

Plas Mawr, Conway:
chimney piece, 1580

This 'multitude of chimneys' was itself a symbol of increasing comfort: it meant that houses were getting warmer. The coal from the many pits sunk during the reign went into the manor house as well as the forge or dye-house, and the great logs that roared between the fire-dogs were aiding and abetting industry to deplete the forests. The chimney, and the chimney piece that answered it indoors, not only offered boundless scope for the display of individual fancy, and so helped to give Elizabethan houses the charm of variety; they also put an end to the day when (in Harrison's words) 'each one made his fire against a reredos in the hall, where he dined and dressed his meat'. The old dark and smoke-filled hall was turning into a reception and dining room where there was light and comfort, and cooking had to accommodate itself to separate quarters. In the best houses even the dining quarters were walled off. Another minor revolution contributing to the same effect was in windows, which need no longer be high and small now that defence had ceased to be a prime consideration; at the same time the importation of glass made possible its use in windows in place of the half-opaque horn of earlier in the century or the still more primitive shutters which left you the choice between excluding the light or letting in the wind and rain. Yet it was masons trained in an older and native tradition that made the framework, and the lovely windows of Tudor country houses remain characteristically English.

The approach to the upper rooms was no longer by narrow winding stone steps, but by a broad and gracious stairway, giving further scope to the wood carver's art. It often terminated now in a long gallery—not yet a picture gallery, since pictures were too few to need one, but a sort of promenade deck where the ladies could stroll and gossip on wet days, the children play at skittles or blind man's buff and their elder brothers and sisters escape match-making parents to pursue their own intrigues. Even a moderate-sized country house like Moreton Hall, near Nantwich, incorporates this feature.

A further contribution to light and warmth was the spread of wainscoting and plaster ceilings. The traditional form of wall decoration, in houses as in churches, had been the painting in tempera or 'water-work', usually by local craftsmen, of texts, 'posies' or religious symbols, arabesques or floral designs, or occasionally more elaborate pictorial efforts. The mayor of Oxford, a friend of Shakespeare, who used to stay with him *en route* from London to Stratford, had his house so decorated at a time when richer and more fashionable folk had come to prefer what Falstaff contemptuously called 'fly-bitten tapestries' to the sort of 'pretty slight drollery, or the story of the Prodigal . . . in water-work' that suited Sir John's fancy. But if painted walls were cold and tapestry apt to become fly-bitten, wood was both warm and durable, and the timber wainscot became characteristic of the Elizabethan house. So too with ceilings: the wooden ceiling that had at first divided solar from raftered hall (when bedrooms came in) was now lightened by plaster, with appropriate designs ranging from

Hardwick Hall, Derbyshire: the Long Gallery, c. 1595
(From a late nineteenth-century drawing)

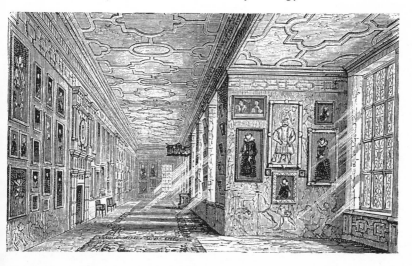

the simplicity of Plas Mawr at Conway to the more elaborate ceilings of Gawthorpe or Speke Hall, in Lancashire. And so plaster co-operated with glass to give light and to make the main entertaining room less of a fortress, more of a home: 'much more close' is Harrison's way of putting it, meaning by 'close' not stuffy, but companionable.

Although timber was being more extensively used inside, as building material it was giving place to brick in most of the newer houses of the south and east; the Londoner who now rebuilt his house in brick earned the thanks of his grandchildren when neighbouring timber houses succumbed to the Great Fire a century later. But wood retained its popularity in the southern midlands, in the borderland and eastern counties of Wales and in woodland areas elsewhere; here the typical Elizabethan house is the familiar 'black-and-white', conforming to contemporary fashions only in chimneys, windows, stairways, doorways and some other details of craftsmanship, and of course in increased size and solidity. Unhewn stone was commoner in the uplands of Wales and the North, except where dressed stone could be plundered from a demolished abbey; here the brick-built house came rather later.

The fashionable Elizabethan gave almost as much care and thought to his garden as to his house. Burghley had four gardens at Theobalds: the great garden, the old and new privy gardens, and the cook's garden for produce. John Gerard, author of the classic *Herball*, planned and superintended both

A formal Elizabethan garden

these and the gardens of his London house. Nothing is more characteristic of the age than its love of flowers, a taste that can develop only when primary wants are satisfied and life is reasonably secure. Every gentleman's house had not only its kitchen garden, but its formal garden of flowers and shrubs 'for delectation sake unto the

eye and their odoriferous savours unto the nose';
and here, in addition to our native flowers,
exotics from America, the Canaries and other
outlandish parts 'do begin to wax so well
acquainted with our soils', says Harrison, 'that
we may almost account them as part of our
commodities': the discovery of the New World
extended our aesthetic as well as our economic
range. The catalogue of plants at Theobalds
which Gerard made for Burghley was the first
such list to be published here, and it is significant
that the second edition gives the flowers their
English as well as their Latin names; the wood-
cuts with which he adorned his *Herball*—most

Common garden thyme

of them borrowed, like so much of the architecture of the house
itself, from the Low Countries—are the earliest accurate botanical drawings we have. Among the new varieties introduced to
the Elizabethan garden are larkspur and laburnum, Christmas
roses, passion flowers and orange blossom.

The revival of the long-neglected cultivation of herbs and
vegetables was even more widespread in its effects. Home-
grown melons, cucumbers, radishes, carrots, turnips, pumpkins,
parsnips and cabbages appeared on the tables of rich and poor
alike, to the great gain of their dietary; the
potato arrived in the course of the reign, but
it had yet to win its way to popularity. The
family medicine chest was also enriched with
a greater variety of 'simples', and the rich
added 'new seeds out of strange countries'. Good
Parson Harrison, our informant on all this,
boasts that even with his 'small ability' he has
been able to raise three hundred varieties in as
many square feet of garden. Similarly the
orchards with which both town and country
abounded were producing unfamiliar fruits like
apricots, peaches, almonds and figs, even
oranges, lemons and capers, as well as a more
abundant harvest (through grafting) of the

Virginia potato

Grafting

immemorial apples, plums, pears, walnuts and filberts. It is in Master Shallow's pleasant Gloucestershire orchard that Falstaff, invited by his host to 'crack a quart' and eat 'a last year's pippin of my own graffing, with a dish of carroways' and another of 'leather-coats' (russets), is brought news of Henry IV's death, and indulges in his pipe-dreams about the new reign.

Town houses as well as country houses had their gardens and orchards; or, if the site left no room for them, the owner would find him a walled garden in some other part of the town, like any city allotment owner of today. Similarly, if an elaborate country-house frontage was precluded by the site, he would content himself with a plain exterior (as in most London houses of the time, in contrast with those of many continental capitals) concealing an interior which could 'receive a duke with his whole train, and lodge them at their ease'. The retail shop-keeper, of course, would have to sacrifice some part of his internal space to setting out wares and meeting his customers, and perhaps his garden to a warehouse or workshop. What was lost in depth might be gained in height: a London merchant's house of the period could rise to four or five storeys, even an Exeter merchant's to three. Here too a respectable Elizabethan weaver's house boasts a hall, two bedrooms and a kitchen besides the shop, with plentiful hangings and cushions; but the hall has also to serve as a bedroom. A joiner in the same city is found living in a one-roomed house, with the bare minimum of furniture.

It was the lower ranks of rural society that in general failed to keep pace with the new luxury. Farmers and yeomen with social ambitions might rebuild in the style of the gentry, but most of their kind preferred to stick to their ancestral clay-and-wattle houses and to spend any surplus from the soil on food. A

Spaniard arriving here in the days of Queen Mary is reputed to have exclaimed 'These English have their houses made of sticks and dirt, but they fare commonly so well as the king.' Single-storey houses were commonest in this social grade, or if there was an 'upstairs' it was a garret or attic approached by ladder. This is how Joseph Hall, the future bishop, describes the small copyholder's house almost at the end of the reign:

> *Of one bay's breadth, God wot, a silly cote*
> *Whose thatched spars are furred with sluttish soot*
> *A whole inch thick, shining like a blackmoor's brows*
> *Through smoke that downe the headless barrel blows,*
> *At his bed's feete, feeden his stalled teame,*
> *His swine beneath, his pullen o'er the beame.*

Of the living conditions of the day-labourer, in town or in country, very little can be said: his 'silly cote'—a sleeping place only, since he worked long hours and fed as he worked—was too flimsy to survive, and he himself too illiterate to leave any personal record, too insignificant to find a place in the public records except when he broke the law. For most purposes, he was still living in the middle ages.

Increasing comfort in the home was not confined to light and heat; the Elizabethans were learning to lie softer. The last generation, Harrison tells us, was content with 'a good round log' for a pillow and lay on straw pallets with a harsh coverlet of rough-woven yarn or woollen shreds; a man was prospering if he had risen to a feather bed within seven years of his marriage. But Elizabeth's was the age of the great four-poster, with its elaborate hangings, pillows, mattresses and coverlets. Shakespeare's

Shakespeare's birthplace, Stratford-upon-Avon

second-best bed, and the formidable array of four-posters claiming to have served the queen on her progresses, have become bywords; even our Exeter joiner, with only £4 worth of goods to his name, included among them a feather bed and bolster. In some rural areas, however, pillows were looked on as effeminate, and the wooden log held its place. Furniture everywhere was scanty, but solid, and made, except in the wealthier families, of native timber by local joiners. Chairs were for the master and mistress and for guests of honour only: stools or benches for the rest. Except in the best houses they were stark and unpadded.

Even in furniture, however, regard for comfort was gaining ground: cushions and stuffs were getting commoner, and the queen's godson, Sir John Harington, found the stools at court too Spartan for his taste, comparing them unfavourably with the easy sitting in a merchant's house. A dining table and a number of presses, cupboards, small tables and chests would complete the furnishing. The extent of their elaboration would naturally depend on the status of the householder. In the great mansion the dining table, the chair of honour and the best bedstead would give scope for employing foreign craftsmen or imported designs to embody the latest fashions. A nobleman might pay 14s. for a stool and three times as much for an upholstered

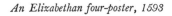

An Elizabethan four-poster, 1593

chair. The furnishing of a moderate-sized country house of the period can be gathered from the inventory of the goods of a Denbighshire gentleman executed for complicity in the Babington plot. The house had twelve bedsteads, ranging in value from 2s. 10d. to £8, and two truckle beds; a dozen sheets (but only four of them linen—the rest probably hempen), half-a-dozen blankets, three bolsters, two vallances (one silk, one fustian), two coverlets and four cushions. The fact that there were five tablecloths and only two towels may throw some light on the frequency of ablutions. A Norfolk knight's house a quarter of a century earlier has half as many bedsteads, the dearest of them worth only £1, three feather beds, and, so far as can be seen, but one pair of blankets. Lower in the social scale the table would be a plain board on trestles, with what decoration the local carpenter could supply from his accustomed patterns, and the beds truckle or 'trussing' beds such as were provided for the maids in superior households. Rushes were the usual floor covering; where carpets were imported (for we had not yet learned to make them for ourselves) they were normally used as hangings or coverings. The humbler home was of course devoid not only of floor coverings but of the flooring itself, possibly to the advantage of its hygiene: though household books suggest that in well-regulated houses the rushes were changed monthly, and not, as is so often alleged, left to fester under a new layer.

On the general sanitary arrangements in these fine houses the less said the better. The queen herself installed at Richmond a water closet newly devised by her godson, but her subjects, high and low alike, were unimpressed by the invention. The rich man might rise to the luxury of an indoor 'house of easement', even of covering the seat with baize; he might spend four or five shillings on 'chaumber pottes' for the household; but his methods of sewage disposal were basically as primitive as those of the humblest cottager. Luckily he had plenty of room to avoid the immediate danger of pestilence that stalked in the train of insanitary habits in the narrow streets of populous towns or overgrown villages. Baths were a simple matter: they could be taken, if at all, by the gentry in front of their bedroom fires with sweet herbs to scent the water, by the cottager in the pond or river. Soap was not lacking, even scented soap, although the chief constituent was wood ash. The exotic luxury of Turkish baths had just been introduced when Harrison wrote, though he does not call them by that name. There was no need to worry about trifles like the emptying of bath tubs and privy tubs when service was plentiful and cheap for the upper classes, and in the lower middle and lower classes the housewife accepted these duties as part of the lot to which God had called her.

Among the other changes which impressed Harrison's 'oldest inhabitant' was the greater refinement of table-ware: the substitution, for example, of silver, pewter or tin vessels for wooden ones and the use of 'Venice glasses' for drinking. Such an expert as Falstaff himself thought 'glasses, glasses is the only drinking'. Our own efforts in glass-blowing were not yet successful enough to bring within reach of the rank and file anything better than rough glass manufactured from 'fern and stone', but Sheffield saw to it that knives were plentiful enough; a guest often brought his own to table. Forks were still a rarity: hence the need for a ewer of water on the table for washing greasy hands between courses. Harrison rejoices that even 'inferior artificers and many farmers' are learning to 'garnish their cupboards with plate, their joined beds with tapestry and silk hangings, and their tables with carpets and fine napery'.

Plate, after all, was an investment as well as an adornment, and an acceptable one in pre-banking days; for land, the only other important form of wealth, could not be turned into money at short notice, and few were hardy enough, like Bess of Hardwick, to keep four great chests of coin in their bed-chambers. Even wholesale merchants conducted most of their transactions by direct barter or by bills of exchange. When the hostess of the Boar's Head in Eastcheap swore she would have to pawn her plate if Falstaff defaulted in the hundred marks he owed her for food and drink, she was only indicating the practice of her betters. It was the common resort of the nobility and gentry when they were faced with the need for

large sums down to finance a lawsuit, an adventure in arms or
afloat, the purchase of a profitable office or the expenses of an
unpaid one—even so prosaic a call as the demands of the tax
gatherer. Walsingham's stepson Christopher Carleill, adventurer and explorer, pawned his collection of plate for £400,
and died before he could redeem it; the seventh earl of Shrewsbury, at odds with his family and his own tenants and needing
abundant cash to fight them all, had over £1,000 worth of
jewels in pawn for five years, till the crisis subsided.

Food and clothes offered further scope for luxury. Exuberance
in dress matched exuberance in architecture, and showed
something of the same determination to be what Samuel
Rowland called 'the world's ape of fashion', but it also affected
as limited a range of society:

> . . . the French doublet and the German hose;
> The Muffs cloak, Spanish hat, Toledo blade,
> Italian ruff, a shoe right Flemish made

were rarely seen in the country town, never in the village, nor
yet among city merchants unless perhaps when they appeared
at court. 'Certes', concedes the puritanical Harrison, after a
tirade against extravagance in dress, jewels and even beards,
'of all estates our merchants do least alter in their attire'; yet
the civic fathers had everywhere to be on the alert to prevent the
sober citizen from aping the courtier,
and to restrict display in dress to the
right occasions and the proper social
grades. The impact of fashion on the
urban middle classes was less in the
colour or cut than in the quality of
the cloth they wore; for thanks to the
settlement of skilled foreigners in
Norwich and elsewhere fine cloth could
now be had at home. Foreign hats were
perhaps their chief sartorial adventure:
the native capper was having a thin

'I wyl were I cannot tel what'
Satire on craze for novelty in dress

65

'Velvet breeches and cloth breeches'

time. The wilder flights of fashion did not touch the ordinary country gentleman in his clothes any more than in his lodging, and the yeoman and farmer stuck to their homespun broadcloth and their native dyes of 'brown, blue or . . . sad tawny' which to Harrison were the true hallmarks of 'merry England'; while the peasant and the poor artisan, if not literally 'hempen homespuns', wore Surrey or Hampshire kerseys or the 'cottons' (in which the wool was 'cottoned' with teasles) made in Lancashire, Cheshire and central Wales, outside the scope of the regulations applied by gild or government to finer grades of cloth, and used by their betters as linings.

Luxury in food spread rather more widely, because it was less dependent on foreign imports. The rich nobleman's table, in its pomp and circumstance as well as in the richness and variety of its dishes, fell little if any behind the royal court. Master Shallow's idea of a modest repast, it will be remembered, was 'a couple of short-legg'd hens, a joint of mutton, and any pretty little tiny kickshaws'. A better idea of the daily fare of a country gentleman of some £2,000 a year can be gathered from the detailed accounts of William Darrell, a Wiltshire squire of frugal tastes, during three months of 1589 when he was detained in London lodgings, with a skeleton staff of servants,

Court-lady and country-woman

over a tangle of lawsuits. Beef and mutton (whole joints, of course) are his staple dishes at both dinner and supper; there are also side dishes of game—a brace or more of pullets, rabbits, or occasionally pheasants and pigeons —sometimes of veal, once of lamb. Bread and beer are always there, and often butter and cheese, but soup (or 'broth') and 'sallets' are surprisingly rare, and peas

66

seem to be the only vegetable. For sweets, the usual pasties and jellies do not interest him, but in season he has an occasional quart of strawberries, sometimes with cream. Friday is normally, but by no means always, a

A bachelor dinner-party

fish day, with ling, plaice, whiting or conger (herring or salt fish on leaner days) taking the place of the joint. The law enjoining two fish days a week evidently cut little ice with him. Breakfast—of eggs—only once comes into the picture. Almost the only exotics that appear are oranges and lemons and a very rare pint of claret. The cost of each meal ranged between five and ten shillings—not a very high proportion of his income. Both fare and cost approximate to those of a 'gaudy' dinner at an Oxford college of the day; but compare them with the lawyer's 'ordinary' which cost threepence.

Darrell's, of course, were solitary dinners, and Shallow's a bachelor party. A family meal was a more formidable business, each 'course' consisting of a full dinner as we understand it today. Nor was the wealthy city merchant behind, if we may trust the imaginary dialogues, in English and French interleaved, composed by two Huguenot refugees to teach city children French. Here the choice of dishes includes a leg of mutton stuffed with garlick, a venison pasty eaten with sugared mustard, a capon boiled with leeks, roasted blackbirds, larks, woodcocks, partridges, a hare, a shoulder of veal, and salted beef 'as tender and shorte as veneson'; for vegetables turnips and cabbage—unhappily over-seasoned, so that father has to forgo his favourite dish of cabbage; for fish, stewed carp and pike with 'high Dutch' sauce; roasted pears, apples and 'scrapped cheese' for dessert; and several sorts of wines, which have to be replenished at the tavern before the meal is over. Table linen is abundant; cutlery less so. Probably some of the dishes are introduced for purposes of vocabulary; but Harrison

A family meal

confirms that the merchant fares as well as the gentleman, as well even as the nobleman on high days and holidays. His disapproval of extravagance does not extend to food: the multitude of dishes, he explains, enables each guest to choose his particular fancy, and no one normally consumes more than half-a-dozen of them on guest days, or two or three *en famille*. Besides, what is over goes to supplement the basic 'diets' of the household staff, and a gentleman must at all costs be open-handed. Rarely does a dish reappear on the table, unless it be an occasional cold joint for supper.

Harrison will not have it that gentlemen habitually over-eat or over-drink; it is the 'meaner sort of husbandman' who guzzles and becomes 'cupshotten' at public feasts to compensate for long weeks of broth and porridge, dairy produce, the inevitable bacon and rye or barley bread, with beer, cider or mead according to the district, and perhaps butcher's meat for Sunday dinner. The townsman's diet differed little from that of his country cousin, for he too usually kept a pig, as harassed officials knew to their cost. Only in times of famine in the country or unemployment in the town was he reduced to making do with bread of dried peas or acorns.

In town, dinner was normally at noon, supper at five; in

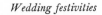

Wedding festivities

the country an hour or two earlier, and here harvesters and haymakers in the busy season took their bread and cheese, apple pasty and beer or cider out to the fields to be consumed at the appropriate pause. Children in better-class homes had their meals separately, with a good foundation of porridge, but one of the sons might be brought in to salute the guests and to say grace, even to read a passage of

Infancy

scripture to them: for the art of conversation was not highly cultivated in Elizabethan England. Breakfast was not a family meal: those who took it (and not all did) had it in their rooms. There was a merciful pause between meals, and generally an ample staff to cope with them. The officials in a great lord's household matched in numbers, dignity and often in name those of the queen's court; even in a rich bourgeois home like those portrayed in our Anglo-French dialogues we read of a steward to superintend the household, at least one cook, a lacquey and chamberlain to look after the children, a page or pages to wait at table, and countless unnamed underlings who flit about in the background. In the country there would have to be an outdoor staff as well. Their money wages need not amount to much. William Darrell's annual wage bill, when he was at home in Wiltshire, only came to £50 all told. In a more modest merchant household two or three maids, including the children's nurse, would suffice, their wages ranging downwards from £4 a year, according to skill and responsibility; and the food bill might be in the region of 30s. a week. But of course money wages were only part of their takings. Clothes or liveries were provided, to say nothing of their 'diets' and the unwanted dishes that went to them from the family table. A merchant like Thomas Myddelton in his early days, dealing wholesale in both cloth and groceries, could supplement domestic wages by sending to his warehouse for dress lengths or provisions, and domestic service itself by using his office staff in times of crisis like childbirth, when he personally, in default of a steward, took charge of the household.

Over these households, large or small, the father presided with regal authority: more than regal in some respects, since he had all his subjects under his eye. It was no sinecure for him or his consort. The family itself might well include the children of two or three marriages, and married sons or daughters, with wives and husbands, who had not yet set up for themselves. Much of his time and thought were spent on delicate negotiations with fellow-potentates on the marriage of the other children. And if he was in this way his own foreign minister and head of the treasury, he delegated to his wife, apart from her special domains of the brewhouse and stillroom, the duties of chancellor of the exchequer and minister of the interior. On her fell the immediate responsibility for seeing that the household, family and retainers alike, held together both as an economic and as a social unit: as one of those interlocking cells, in fact, that gave the Elizabethan state its solid basis and its life and character. Both alike did in the long run tend to hold together, despite all internal revolts and external jars, whether wars or lawsuits: the one by the bond of family pride, if not family affection, which permeated a well-run household, the other through the patriotism fostered by the intuitive wisdom of the queen.

In the microcosm of the home these jars might arise from the family itself or from the household staff. For the former there were unwritten laws of family honour to back paternal authority; for the latter written laws might be imposed, with fines, flogging and the threat of dismissal as sanctions, and

A mother with her children

A deathbed scene

very little hope, as there was in the wider community, of finding escape in flight. What if the page waiting at table made the host a laughing-stock to his guests by taking a sly sip from the wine bottle behind his chair of state? What if a kitchen-hand sucked the gravy from a pie before bringing it to table? What if the meal itself was late, the service or the servants slovenly or negligent? In a Somerset household, where the master as high sheriff had a special dignity to maintain, fines ranging from a penny for swearing or slatternly dress and twopence for absence from family prayers, to sixpence for the most heinous offence of all, unpunctuality in serving dinner, were deducted every quarter day from wages, along with the cost of breakages. The list invites comparison with a similar one posted in a Surrey household nearly two centuries later: the range of fines is much the same, except for an overriding five shillings imposed on anyone defacing the list; but absence from family prayers, if any, no longer brings a penalty, nor does swearing except at meals, and the sixpenny fine is limited to offences such as letting dogs lick the plates. Cleanliness had by then triumphed over godliness. Otherwise life below stairs, or its equivalent, shows the same unchanging constancy, as long as it persists, as the peasant's diet and dress.

Further Reading

CONTEMPORARY

The Elizabethan Home. Discovered in Two Dialogues by Claudius Hollyband and Peter Erondell (ed. M. St. C. Byrne; illustrated), 1930.

LATER

E. Burton, *The Elizabethans at Home* (illustrated), 1958.

H. Hall, *Society in the Elizabethan Age* (illustrated), 1901.

J. Lees-Milne, *Tudor Renaissance* (illustrated), 1951.

V

The Church

Of all those interlaced communities that made up Tudor society, none, hardly even the family, was more pervasive than the church. From time immemorial its local unit, the parish, had been the centre of a vigorous communal life radiating from the parish church, and impressing itself at every stage of the parishioner's journey from cradle to grave. It was still so in Elizabeth's day. The parish had its own corporate being, even its own corporate funds administered by its own elected churchwardens. These were built up from legacies and supplemented from time to time by self-imposed church rates or voluntary efforts like 'church ales'—the counterpart of the modern church bazaar. When the Reformation swept away the discredited minor orders in the church, one remained: the office of parish clerk; although no longer a 'clerk' in the medieval sense, this parochial man-of-all-work still wore his black gown and still had some ecclesiastical offices to perform, such as reading lessons and leading responses, as well as his increasing load of secular duties, which in a small parish might well include those of beadle and sexton. The parish had its social occasions too—the holy days and their vigils, above all the patronal festival. These were now sadly depleted: Harrison says from ninety-five to twenty-seven. Holy-days meant idleness, and national strength and independence, so often threatened in these days of rising Great Powers, could be maintained only by increased home production. Yet much remained. There was Plough Monday and Mothering Sunday, Shrovetide with its traditional football and its licensed horseplay among scholars and apprentices, less exuberant versions of the continental Carnival and Mardi Gras; there was Hallowe'en and the beating of the bounds at Rogation-tide,

A village festival

and of course the parochial Wakes. All of them showed remarkable power of weathering successive bans; and no one had succeeded in seriously abridging the twelve days of Christmas merrymaking from which Plough Monday sounded the recall to labour in the fields.

In some ways Tudor policy made the parish more important than ever before. Thomas Cromwell had turned the parson into a registrar of births, marriages and deaths; Queen Mary had wished upon the parish a new official, the surveyor of highways, elected to take his turn for a year, without payment, at directing the reluctant and not very effective efforts of his fellow-parishioners towards filling in ruts and pot-holes in the parish roads. The parish had always looked after its own poor in its own fashion, but Elizabeth added yet another bevy of statutory officials, the overseers of the poor, selected by the county magistrates from among substantial parishioners to relieve the churchwardens in the discharge of this task and to help them out in other ways. For the wardens, and of course the parson with them, were also now charged with a growing burden of civil duties. The petty constable, whose job was the maintenance of order, was still a manorial official appointed in court leet, but offences which could be regarded as moral and not merely legal fell within the province of the wardens, whose obligation it was to see that the offenders were brought before the bishop's court; above all, they must see that all the parish attended divine worship, and that alehouses were not open during service hours to lure them away. As long as slackness in churchgoing was just a matter of ordinary human frailty, this was simple enough; everyone knew who were the village reprobates. But by Elizabeth's time the absentee might be a man of substance who declined on principle to conform to the changes in worship which queen and parliament had

73

decreed; and as religious strife grew more intense in the middle years of the reign, and the penalties for 'recusancy' correspondingly heavier, the warden became not only a parish policeman but an inquisitor with the unpleasant task of spying on his neighbours, and liable to even more unpleasant consequences if he failed to come up to scratch.

There was no escaping these parish offices, unless one was prepared to pay a heavy fine; nor were there any emoluments attached. The one consolation was that at the next Easter vestry someone else would have to take over; so the important thing was to get through the year with the minimum of offence to superiors on the one hand and neighbours on the other. The parish vestry, where all these elections were made, was in name a meeting of the whole body of parishioners, not just of free tenants of the manor, like the court leet. But naturally in practice, and often by formal consent of the parish, attendance was limited to some dozen or two of the leading parishioners, with the parson in the chair and the wardens to support him. All manner of parish business came before it, from the upkeep of the church fabric, for which the vestry could levy a rate and distrain on defaulters, to the ravages of vermin and the condition of the roads. It was a veritable parish parliament.

Yet in essence the parish was much more than an organ of civil government: it was an association of worshippers; and many, many bewildering changes in the form of worship had been prescribed by authority during the half-century before the queen's accession. The successive shifts of allegiance from Pope to Supreme Head, from Supreme Head back to Pope, from Pope to Supreme Governor, were matters over which only the more knowledgeable vexed themselves. Rome was far off; their grandfathers had heard whispers of worse than this when rival popes thundered excommunications against each other, and they themselves had seen Queen Mary's catholic restoration hampered by a pope politically hostile to Spain. They had also seen of late an unwontedly rapid turnover of bishops, and that came a little nearer home—though bishops were often away on state service, or even permanent absentees. Mary's reign had brought with it wholesale deprivations or resignations of the parish priests themselves, and even the burning of some of them at the stake; and although the great mass of ordinary churchgoers had no doubt welcomed the restoration of the old Latin services and vestments after the iconoclasm of Edward VI's day, the reign had ended in disappointment and gloom,

The Cathedral Church of London: Old St Paul's

for it had brought the deep humiliation of the loss of Calais, our last footing on the continent.

So the new reign started in hope, even with a sigh of relief. Most of the Marian priests remained at their posts, in contrast with almost a clean sweep of the bench of bishops. The repudiation of the papacy for the second time in fifty years caused relatively little stir; the queen at least toned down the title her father had assumed, and the public was reassured that a woman was not going to try to play the pope over them. And if she was hustled by Marian exiles, back home from Germany or Switzerland with advanced protestant ideas, into reimposing sooner than she planned an English service book, that too was toned down from the version her brother had prescribed. Besides, it was likely to be some time before the new bishops got into their stride, and most of the priests who remained in their parishes could be trusted to cling as long as they could to the accustomed order, directives from Westminster or Canterbury notwithstanding. And so it proved. When in 1562 the Book of Homilies was published for reading in churches, by far the longest of them—over six times as long as any other— was Bishop Jewel's homily against Peril of Idolatry, castigating to the tune of a hundred pages the 'spiritual fornication', as he calls it, obviously still common everywhere: 'our churches stand full of such great puppets, wondrously decked and adorned; garlands and coronets be set on their heads, precious stones hanging about their necks; their fingers shine with rings set with precious stones; their dead and stiff bodies are clothed with garments stiff with gold'.

That this homily, with its learned references to ecclesiastical history, was ever inflicted in its entirety on any congregation, even in instalments, as suggested by authority, is hard to believe. If so, it certainly cut little ice in strongholds of conservatism like Wales and the North. Five years later royal commissioners in Yorkshire were still struggling manfully to carry out, against strong local opposition, the queen's injunctions for the removal of images, and in many parishes there the passing bell was rung at Hallowtide, with the usual junketings, even in the next decade. The bishops of Bangor and St. Asaph were battling with 'superstitious uses' in their dioceses under a special royal mandate twenty years after the queen's accession, and even after the Armada, reports kept coming in from remote parishes in this area of the continued use of rosaries in church and of widespread resort and deference to the shrines of popular saints.

For the first ten or twelve years of the reign, those who disliked the changes in worship could still nurse the hope that things would change again; the sexton at St. David's cathedral was found in 1571 to have hidden away 'mass books, hymnals, grails and such like (as it were looking for a day)'. Until that day came, most people felt that no great harm could come of an occasional bowing in the temple of Rimmon to humour so well-liked a queen. Their very confessors, such as Lord Montague's, sometimes assured them, for all that the fathers at Trent had said, that it was 'expedient something to give to the tyme' and that they 'durst not determine such a fact to be sinne'. A Monmouthshire lawyer who afterwards, as Father Augustine Baker, became a devoted Benedictine, puts the situation as his parents saw it in a nutshell: 'At the first . . . the greatest part even of those who in their judgments and affections had before bin Catholickes, did not well discern any great fault, novelty, or difference from the former religion . . . in this new sett up by Queen Elizabeth, save only change of language. . . . And so easily accommodated themselves thereto.' For such as could not so readily 'accommodate themselves' it was still possible now and then to hear mass in secret from some extruded Marian priest lurking in the neighbourhood. Absence from church only meant a shilling fine, and there was not yet any prescribed penalty for hearing mass. Failing this, one could always console one's self with the old Latin devotions at home, as Baker's parents did.

The greatest weakness of the Elizabethan settlement was the poverty in which successive spoliations had left the church, a poverty from which the gentry and nobility gained doubly, since on the one hand so much of the spoil had gone into their coffers (and was still pouring into them in the form of impropriate tithe), and on the other it served to keep the clergy in their place, dependent on the gentry. So deeply ingrained was this habit of mind, a lasting reaction from the days when the nobility writhed under the arrogance of low-born Wolseys, that even the Romanist priests who served their flocks in eighteenth-century England suffered from it, and to the gentry who sailed out to colonial America it remained an ark of the covenant which no English metropolitan dared touch.

William Harrison, who, sound protestant as he was, deplored these conditions, reckoned that out of a normal living of £20 a year (half the sum on which Goldsmith's village parson passed as rich) 'the incumbent thinketh himself well acquitted if, all ordinary payments being discharged, he may reserve thirteen pounds six shilling eightpence towards his own sustenation or maintenance of his family'. No wonder it was hard to find university men to compete for these pittances. 'There be few', Bishop Latimer had seen as early as Edward VI's reign, 'do study divinity; for their livings be so small, and victuals so dear, that they tarry not there', leaving the benefices to be filled (in Harrison's jaundiced recital) by 'bakers, butlers, cooks, good archers, falconers, and horsekeepers' of the gentry who presented them—by Sir Oliver Martexts, in fact. The alternative was to return to one of the abuses that had given the Reformation its initial impulse by seeking license to hold several livings together, and sending some bucolic and bibulous hedge priest as curate to the parishes the vicar could not get around.

Clerical marriage presented a problem in itself. Parishioners were used enough to priests who kept their unofficial wives in decent obscurity, but for the vicar openly to set up an establishment like his neighbours, and to try to educate a brood of children appropriately to his station, not only imposed a further strain on his resources, but left his wife with a painfully ambiguous status in parish society; many may have felt what the queen is dubiously alleged to have said in taking leave of the archbishop's wife herself after dining at Lambeth: '*Madam* I may not call you, and *Mistris* I am ashamed to call you, so I know not what to call you.' It may in the long run have helped parish relations to have a parson who understood the family troubles of his flock, but the immediate effect was disturbing; so too was the tendency of parsons to go about dressed like ordinary laymen, and the long reluctance of many of them to wear the prescribed vestments even in church.

Religious instruction in the home

78

THE CHURCH

Take an odd vicar in a village town,
  That only prays for plenty and for peace,
If he can get him but a threadbare gown,
  And tythe a pig, and eat a goose in grease,
  And set his hand unto his neighbour's lease
And bid the clerk on Sundays ring the bell,
  He is a churchman fits the parish well:

Nicholas Breton's description is not wide of the mark for the makeshift parsons of the beginning of the reign; it was becoming less true by the time he wrote, at the end of the century. But even well on in the next reign a Roman Catholic writer describes the clergy of his day as wearing below the cap and rochet 'ruffs much like merchants, but not altogether as large: as for jerkins, doublets, breeches and suchlike', he adds, 'many of the ministers make them after the newest fashion taken up, as the laymen do'.

The apparatus for worship was equally open to criticism, from friend and foe alike. It was Bishop Jewel who exclaimed, 'It is sin and shame to see so many churches ruinous, and so foully decayed', and exhorted parishioners 'to keep your churches comely and clean', with a no doubt necessary reminder that 'it is the house of prayer, not the house of talking, of walking, of brawling, of minstrelsy, of hawks, of dogs'. The complaints of the congregation are often from a different angle. 'Alas, gossip', runs a conversation quoted in one of the Homilies, 'what shall we do now at church, since all the saints are taken away, since all the goodly sights we were wont to have are gone, since we cannot hear the like piping, singing, chanting and playing upon the organ, that we could before?' A schoolmaster of the Welsh borderland, who sealed with his life the faith to which he had been converted by one of the Jesuit missionaries, laments in popular Welsh verse the empty niches where the saints had stood, the 'sorry trestle' that does duty for altar; he lashes the tradesmen turned parsons for 'guzzling flesh and filling the paunch on Fridays, and letting belief revolve with the wind', for 'donning baggy trunks, lying long

79

abed and singing nonsense ditties to the baby', at the same time 'denying wax for lights, burning images and debasing the honour of holy-days'. In more poetic vein an Anglesey bard, a little earlier, is as caustic about the parson's silks and furs (on £20 a year!) as the protestant Harrison is over the popish priests whom he compares to 'a peacock that spreadeth his tail when he danceth before the hen'; and he tells in moving lines his nostalgia for the broken altars, the wax and votive candles, the fragrant incense and 'oil that was balm to the soul'; 'dead cold is our age', he mourns, 'there is blue ice in our churches'.

Not all churchgoers were weathercocks, however, nor were they all nostalgic 'church papists' or occasional conformists; and the number of out-and-out recusants before 1570 was still small. Since the late middle ages there had been a widespread urge for church reform, not merely in the negative sense of the removal of gross abuses in high places (which had been pretty completely, though belatedly, carried out before Elizabeth's reign got under way), but constructively in the direction of a more evangelical faith, resting itself less on the sacraments of the church, more on the scriptures, read in the mother tongue and in the light of personal experience. 'Gospellers', Sir Thomas More had called men of this way of thinking, and the name stuck.

Under Edward VI they had got the upper hand; and nearly five hundred of them had left in an organised body for the continent as soon as Mary succeeded him. They were now back in England, with a strong representation in parliament and among the new bishops; for the queen, little as she liked their ideas, found in them the strongest support for her ecclesiastical supremacy. They only just failed to impress their views on convocation; in parliament the queen was throughout her reign fighting a running battle with them, and sometimes, especially at first, even she had to yield or at least to compromise. What is more immediately to the point, they were represented in almost every English shire and even some of the Welsh ones. Naturally the migration had been heavily concentrated in London and the half-dozen home counties, to the extent of nearly twenty per cent. A dozen midland shires sent not much more than half as many as these; the four seagoing shires of the south-western peninsula sent almost as many as the whole of the north, including all Yorkshire and right down to Lancashire and Cheshire. East Anglia was not far behind them. Some five per cent came from the seventeen shires of Wales and the border, and the three southern seaboard shires, including Southampton and the Isle of Wight, brought up the rear. This gives some slight clue to the regional distribution of those who might be expected to take the lead in active and not merely passive acceptance of the religious changes of the reign, and very broadly that is how it worked out.

Acute divisions had appeared among the gospellers in exile; they were to reappear during those critical middle years of the reign. But on their first return they were united in backing up in their various parishes the authority of bishops and royal commissioners in sweeping away the effects of Mary's religious reaction. For many (including, as soon appeared, Elizabeth herself) this meant little more than returning to the order that prevailed under Henry VIII, so far as conditions now allowed it; but the gospellers looked for a return to the heyday of their power under Edward VI, and a more advanced wing, soon to be labelled 'puritan', already yearned for the use of that position as a springboard for further advance. What brought matters to a head was the series of crises beginning with the flight to England of Mary, queen of Scots, and the succession of plots centring on her as catholic claimant to the throne, and culminating in the Spanish Armada. In between came the most critical event of all, the papal excommunication of the queen in 1570, absolving her subjects from obedience, and the consequent missions of the Jesuits and seminary priests to win them back to Rome. As Augustine Baker put it, 'matters came to be more discerned and digested concerning religion': the easy compromises of the early years of the reign were no longer possible, though many were slow to accept the fact. The recusants gradually became a distinct body in each parish, subject to increasing measures of persecution which their neighbours had to help in enforcing under spasmodic pressure from above dictated by the pressure of events themselves. To a generation versed in the ways of the modern police state the scene is only too familiar: a neighbour or casual passer-by sees muffled figures entering a house, or hears strange sounds issuing from it, at dead of night; he suspects a secret mass, and carries his tale

Martyrdom of Catholic priests

to the authorities; there follow prison, confiscation, perhaps even torture or death.

For such as were not converted by the papal missionaries, the decisive event was the broadcasting of the English Bible. It had been chief objective of 'gospellers' long before the Tudors came in. Henry VIII had whetted their appetites by putting up English Bibles in churches, and then had baulked them by withdrawing from the 'lower orders' permission to read them: 'I prey God amende this blyndnes', a shepherd had scrawled on the flyleaf of a chronicle he bought when the ban came into force. For there can be no doubt at all of the reality of a widespread urge to read the scriptures in English, an urge strong enough in itself to prompt many to learn their letters. What was significant about the Elizabethan restoration of the English Bible was that it was the gospellers exiled in Geneva who brought back with them their own annotated translation, the work of Knox, Coverdale and others, printed for them there in quarto, and conveniently divided, for the first time, into verses; and after some hesitation the queen allowed it to be reprinted and sold by her own printer, first in folio only, then in quarto. Those who wished to study it need no longer throng eagerly but fearfully round church lecterns to hear the gospel spelled out by the best-lettered among them: the family Bible had arrived, and it at once assumed the function it retained at least till Victorian days, that of a register of family births. What is more, the issue of an octavo edition in 1579 brought the Geneva translation within everyone's reach, and England became, in J. R. Green's memorable phrase, the people of a book, and that book the Bible.

The Geneva Bible of 1560

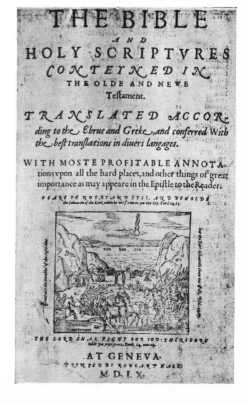

The earlier versions of Henry VIII's reign were frequently reissued, both in folio for church use and in family Bible form, but the Geneva version had got in first and it kept its popularity in the home until it was superseded, slowly, by the James I version; on an average it was reprinted every other year until 1611, our first and longest-lived best-seller. Even the James I version took some time to displace it: a metrical psalter printed seventeen years later

83

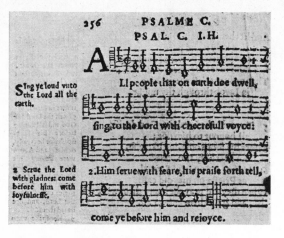

The 'Old Hundredth', from the 1628 edition of an Elizabethan psalter

adds in the margin the psalms in prose according to the Geneva version.

It was an event of immeasurable consequence. Bible-reading became a normal family habit, as it still was in Victorian times. In country houses the chaplain might regale the family with it while they strolled up and down the long gallery; in bourgeois families, as we have seen, the youngsters were sometimes brought in to read it while their elders dined; partly, perhaps, to show off their prowess, partly to make up for lack of conversation. In any case it sank, as we all know, into the language. It did more than that. The Geneva marginal annotations—Calvinistic in tone, of course—gave the ordinary Englishman his first real taste of controversial theology. This was just what both Elizabeth and her father before her had wanted to avoid: they knew enough about the continent (which the average Englishman did not) to be fully awake to what religious controversy might mean. Up to now the doctrinal element in the English Reformation had been negligible: both Henry and his daughter had contented themselves with reasserting the basic creeds of the universal church, and Elizabeth firmly resisted the pressure of the gospellers in parliament to reissue the articles of belief of her brother's reign. At last she was driven by papal onslaughts from 1570 onwards to consent to a definition of the official faith of the English church, and the Thirty-Nine Articles followed next year. Like everything else about the Elizabethan *régime* they were a compromise; what she firmly resisted to the end of the reign was pressure both from parliament and from most of the bishops to impose on the church a rigidly Calvinistic creed.

If the scriptures were read, they must be expounded; that was common ground to all: queen, parliament, bishops, gospellers of all shades. Puzzled parishioners must have their doubts cleared up, and ignorance on basic truths must be dispelled; even more important from the point of view of government, respect for the social order must be maintained. Hence, as an immediate expedient, the Book of Homilies. The demand for more regular sermons had grown concurrently with the demand for the Bible in English. But there were difficulties. To begin with, competent preachers were in short supply, a weakness in the church which puritans went on denouncing for the next hundred years. By extremists such importance was attached to the sermon ('God's instrument of salvation' in Latimer's view) as the mainspring of the service that they doubted if a 'dumb' minister were a true minister at all, at whose hands communion might be received. But the growing interest in dogma raised another obstacle: what if the pulpit should become a platform for religious, and hence, inevitably, political controversy? What if readers failed to find in their Bibles sanction for institutions or ceremonies enjoined by law, and concluded that the Bible must have the last word? What if they suited the deed to the Word and set up their own presbyterian organisation, with the co-operation of the local clergy and in defiance of the bishops, as happened over wide areas in the 1580s?

Here the queen decisively interposed her royal supremacy: no unlicensed preaching! But that again offended puritan sentiment, for how could the preacher proclaim the oracles of God if he was hedged about with caveats by queen and bishops? In Wales there was a further complication: English, whether read from the Bible or preached from the pulpit, was unintelligible to most of the people, so there must be a Welsh Bible and Welsh sermons. But the language, rich in poetic diction and metre, had in prose advanced little beyond simple narrative. A Welsh version of the Bible was decreed by Act of Parliament in 1563 and, after several

'Godly Zeal pluck'd out of his pulpit'

false starts, achieved a quarter of a century later. Eventually it perhaps did more for Wales even than the English Bible did for England, but Wales had to wait over fifty years for a portable edition answering to the Geneva octavo of 1579. Hence, in part, the slow development of puritanism there, except where it seeped in from the border or was brought by sea to Pembrokeshire from Bristol or London. But the Welsh Prayer Book had appeared in 1567; it did wonders towards reconciling the country to the Elizabethan settlement, in marked contrast with what happened on the other side the Irish Sea, where the work of translation was attempted too late.

The influence of the Bible did not end here. Constant reading of the Old Testament tended to prolong the medieval habit of mind which saw in material success or failure evidence of divine favour or displeasure, and was always prepared to meet the supernatural round the next corner. In this sense England remained basically medieval until the scientific age which dawned in the middle of the next century. The assumption was fostered by phrases in both Prayer Book and Homilies; but it was Foxe's *Acts and Monuments*—familiar to us as the Book of Martyrs—that gave it the most direct practical application. The *Acts and Monuments*, published in English in 1564, was much more than a martyrology, though in that aspect it has left a lasting imprint on English character; it was more even than the ecclesiastical history Foxe himself had in mind; the book was an attempt at a philosophy of English history on the basis of the Old Testament and the Book of Revelation. The English are God's chosen people for putting down Antichrist, who is identified with the pope; and victory is assured unless they apostasise as their fathers had from John's submission to the pope until Henry VIII threw off the yoke: that is the gist of it. This identification of the pope with Antichrist, first proclaimed by Wyclif, was encouraged even in the Book of Homilies, though

John Foxe, the martyrologist, 1516–87

happily in none of the church's articles or liturgies. It has much to answer for in English history.

Next to the Bible, Foxe's must have been the most influential religious work of the day. True, a folio of nearly two thousand pages could hardly become a best-seller; but an order of 1571 laid down that copies should be available in all cathedrals and in the houses of the upper clergy and gentry for the use of servants and visitors, and we know that it was kept for the same purpose at the royal court. We know, too, that it was read and retailed, and that it coloured English thought for generations to come. The author of *Euphues* is just as sure that 'the lyving God is onely the English God' as the martyrologist himself; in *Henry the Eighth* even Shakespeare, whose patriotism never sinks to these depths, borrows for Cranmer's messianic prophecy at the christening of Elizabeth the symbol of the vine which stood in Old Testament psalm and prophecy for regenerate and glorified Israel. Religion and patriotism were at one, and in this lies one of the keys to the greatness of the age.

No sooner had the *Acts and Monuments* come from the press than the country was engulfed in that long-drawn crisis which culminated in the Armada's defeat. Within a few years the massacre of Sir John Hawkins's company at San Juan de Ulloa showed the hitherto friendly Don in a new light; the Ridolfi Plot, following the Bull of Excommunication, revealed that he had (as Cromwell put it eighty years later) 'an interest in your bowels', notably among the recusants. He fitted well into Foxe's pattern as an instrument of Antichrist; and there is no reason to doubt that when Drake and his associates spoiled the Egyptians and smote the Amalekite hip and thigh they honestly believed themselves to be God's instruments. It was, appropriately, one of Drake's buccaneers who translated the Psalms into Welsh verse. From this happy harmony of service to God with service to self and country the recusant was excluded. The papal bull faced him with a painful conflict of loyalties. He might hate the Don (many of them did) as heartily as any protestant, but the inner conflict remained, by whatever casuistry he might justify loyalty to the queen and contumacy

The Jesuit Mission, 1580: Campion and Parsons

to Rome; in the eyes of ministers, parliament, people and, to a lesser degree, the queen herself he was always an object of suspicion and fear as a potential 'fifth columnist'. The English were learning to be a humane people, and the Smithfield fires of the last reign had not endeared Bloody Mary to her people; but fear begets cruelty, and the Elizabethan persecutions did not excite the same revulsion among the general public because the victims were done to death not as heretics, but as traitors at a time when national security hung by a thread. To the more fanatical of the puritans they were also idolators to be hewn in pieces before the Lord.

By the end of the reign most parishes had settled down to the new church order. The Elizabethan bishop, whatever his faults, normally lived in his diocese, not, as so often in the middle ages, at court or travelling on secular business, and the diocese benefited from his presence. The incumbent was now generally better educated, and schooled by episcopal visitations into greater seemliness and consistency in the conduct of the service; and Hooker's *Ecclesiastical Polity* had given him a philosophy of Anglicanism which was neither Roman nor Genevan. He might have yearnings for more ceremonial, or for less, and he might take the law into his own hands in either direction if his patron was sympathetic and the bishop not too near at hand; but at least the worst chaos was over. His chief remaining worry was finance. Clerical incomes—the incomes, that is, of those who actually served parishes—certainly did not keep pace with national income during the Elizabethan age or for long after; so that relatively at least the parson was growing poorer at a time when the educational demands on him (the demand for sermons, for example) were getting heavier. His wife, now finding her niche in local society, often helped to eke out his income from her dairy or her hen-run. But it was hard going, and the bishops had not the heart to put a stop to pluralism: indeed they resorted to it freely themselves.

Among his congregation, a generation and more had grown up under the spell of the Prayer Book, and it had come to be widely loved. This, and the association of Rome with Spain and the Armada, helped them to forget their nostalgia for what the Reformation had destroyed. The regular routine of matins at seven (or five in cathedrals) followed by communion and baptisms, and vespers at two, had already established itself as part of the natural order of things: there were few who remembered anything else. Some, no doubt, like the sexton of St. David's were still 'as it were looking for a day', whether the day of Rome or the day of Geneva; either might come in with the queen's successor, so most men were content to go on looking. The recusant who could not reconcile it with his conscience to wait paid his fines as long as his estate would stand it, or went to prison if he was too poor. The advanced puritan was often just as impatient. Many of them felt, as a Pennsylvania quaker put it a century later, that 'the Church of England had settled on her lees since Queen Mary's time', and were all set to continue the interrupted work of 'reformation'; a few had come to think it mortal sin to continue in communion with a church which still bore so many of the marks of Antichrist, and formed their own conventicles, which were treated with as heavy a hand as those of the papist. Some of them too perished as traitors, for they had flouted the queen's supremacy.

The 'judicious' Hooker, c. 1554–1600

The Elizabethan age has often been called secular in tone. It was certainly intent on the pursuit of material wealth, by fair means or by foul. Yet it contrived some sort of synthesis between this and a profound conviction of the divine government of the universe and an honest desire—a preoccupation with many—to ascertain the divine will and

89

to serve as its instruments. The medieval world picture, with its 'chain of being' which linked the angels by infinite gradations to the rocks and reptiles, was still the background of thinking, irrespective of creed or class. In this respect there was no jolt in common ways of thinking for another hundred years.

Further Reading

CONTEMPORARY

An Elizabethan Recusant House (ed. A. C. Southern), 1954.

Latimer, *Sermons* (Everyman's Library), 1906.

The Other Face: Catholic Life under Elizabeth I (ed. P. Caraman), 1960.

LATER

A. G. Dickens, *The English Reformation*, 1964.

C. Hill, *Economic Problems of the Church from Whitgift to the Long Parliament*, 1956.

W. H. Frere, *History of the Church of England*, Vol. V, 1558–1625 (ed. Stephens and Hunt), 1911.

Knappen, *Tudor Puritanism*, 1939.

A. O. Meyer, *England and the Catholic Church under Queen Elizabeth* (trans. McKee), 1916.

The burning of Anabaptists

School and College

The whining schoolboy, with his satchel
And shining morning face, creeping like snail
Unwillingly to school

is among the most familiar and least 'dated' of Shakespearian
characters; but the Elizabethan schoolboy had far more excuse
for this snail's pace than his successor of today. An Elizabethan
had no illusion about schooldays as 'the happiest days of your
life'. Why should they be? Life was hard: best that the young-
ster should learn at an early age, and learn the hard way, to
cope with it. It is true that the most advanced educational
theories of the day, those of Ascham and Mulcaster for example,
were against excessive flogging, but what we know of educational practice does not suggest that their precepts were
widely followed: the birch always figures prominently in
contemporary illustrations of the schoolroom, sometimes even
on school seals. After all, why spare the rod? In the family it
was the normal instrument for inculcating obedience, industry,
manners, religion itself.

The child, it has been said, was in Elizabethan eyes just a
diminutive and exceptionally troublesome adult; it was not
heaven that lay about us in our infancy. Nor was there much
idea of progression, whether in the individual or the community: no one had yet coined the blessed word 'evolution'.
The general belief was rather in cycles of life succeeding each
other, as it were spirally, each repeating the experience of the
last at a different level. The history of the race is not that of an
advancing army, but of an army marching and counter-marching
against an enemy, now captive, now freed again: for long
weary years Satan is loosed on the world, then for just as long

he is in chains. Individual life is not a steady development but a sequence of short lifetimes, each with its rhythm of growth and decay: the seven-year climacteric, or Shakespeare's seven ages—excepting the first, which is barely on the human plane, and the last, which repeats it. 'Degree', the essential basis of society, did not mean a gradation of stepping stones from class to class for the enterprising and worthy, but a series of layers, each a miniature but self-contained society, with escape to the next layer always a possibility, but not an ambition to be encouraged. Even Elizabethan repasts, as we have seen, were a succession of courses each a balanced meal in itself!

So too in education. Elizabethans did not think as we do in terms of an 'educational ladder'; rather each stage of education repeated in a more complex form the content of the last. The lad learning his catechism is introduced to the same circle of ideas as the divinity student at Oxford, with the 'ifs' and 'buts' left out; the university curriculum repeats the grammar school curriculum, but amplifies it; the delinquent student is subject to the same discipline of docked rations, impositions and flogging as the schoolboy; the married man not yet graduated from the parental roof is still under parental discipline with his younger brothers. It is in keeping with all this that the painters of the age should so often portray children and new-born babes as complete but tiny adults, or Shakespeare assure us that the child is father to the man. Perhaps the branch of education of which this is least true is the one to which least attention was devoted in the age of Elizabeth: primary education. So far as it existed, and we really know very little about it in detail, it was not a diluted version of grammar school education but rather an acquisition of the mechanical equipment (reading and writing) without which there could be no formal education at all.

The birch

In medieval times elementary teaching had been part of the job of the chantry priest whose time was otherwise spent on endowed masses for the departed. Either he himself taught or he paid someone to do it for him out of the endowment. In abolishing the chantries as 'superstitious', Henry VIII and the regency which ruled for his son had provided that the educational part of the endowment should continue; in practice the proviso proved impossible to work, especially with an empty exchequer facing the commissioners who carried it out. Local vigilance and pres-

Master and pupil

sure, if necessary the use of local funds where education was highly valued, kept some of these foundations alive or refounded them, but many disappeared. We need not conclude that the obvious need for elementary education was ignored. For the boy going on to the grammar school there had to be some provision, and the parents of this type of lad were as a rule powerful or wealthy enough to see that it was made. Some of the endowed grammar schools met the need by providing elementary classes for such as had not yet learned their letters; sometimes what we should call a separate preparatory school ('petty school' is the Elizabethan term) was set up as part of the endowment; occasionally, as at Manchester Grammar School and a few others, the nineteenth-century monitorial or pupil-teacher system was anticipated to meet this need.

Naturally this business of learning one's letters was often carried out at home, under care of the mother or, in grander households, the tutor or domestic chaplain; he might well be able to go further than this and prepare his charges for the university. The widespread practice among the gentry of sending their sons and sometimes their daughters to board in other gentle households meant that the tutor might have under his charge a miniature private school, especially if he had gained a wider reputation; was not this how in Italy many of the Renaissance academies sprang up? And of course here the pupil would learn much that was not taught in the grammar

From a Latin treatise on swimming

school: a modern language, perhaps, like French or Italian; with young Edward Herbert of Cherbury, born and bred in Shropshire but heir to a Montgomeryshire estate, it was to learn Welsh as well as Greek, Latin, French and Italian that he was sent at nine years old to live in the household of the learned Edward Thelwall, in Denbighshire; though he admits that, 'I did . . . little profit in learning the Welsh, or any other of those languages that worthy gentleman understood.' But there was much more than book-learning to be picked up in a gentleman's, still more in a nobleman's household. Ben Jonson sums it up as

> *. . . letters, arms,*
> *Fair mien, discourses, civil exercises*
> *And all the blazon of a gentleman,*

and he asks

> *Where can he learn to vault, to ride, to fence,*
> *To move his body gracefuller, to speak*
> *His language purer, or to tune his mind*
> *Or manners more to the harmony of nature*
> *Than in these nurserys of nobility?*

It was also a valuable discipline; the page in a noble household was usually of gentle birth himself, and his position may be compared to that of a fag in a modern public school, except that he learned his lessons from a better instructor, and they were possibly more worth learning!

None of this met the case of the labourer, artisan or husbandman who did not aspire to the grammar school for his children but did want them to read the Bible for themselves instead of depending on the verbal instruction of the priest: perhaps to go further and learn to write and cast accounts. How far these mild ambitions could be achieved depended very much on local conditions. In some parishes there were endowments, administered by the churchwardens, under which the parson could add a few pounds to his meagre stipend by keeping school; a very energetic and conscientious incumbent might do it voluntarily. After all it was an obligation on him, laid down in royal injunctions and often emphasised in episcopal visitations, to provide an exhibition at university or grammar school for one lad of promise out of every £100 he earned, and how else could such promise be discovered in parishes where there was no endowed school? On the other hand, how many livings with actual cure of souls brought in as much as £100? So a good deal of this elementary instruction was given in small and ephemeral schools of the type of the Victorian dame school, kept perhaps by the sexton or bell-ringer at a mark a year, or by 'poor women or others whose necessities compel them to undertake it as a mere shelter from beggary'.

There is every indication that schools of this type were widespread even in remote shires, and that many of them went well beyond the rudiments; but only by chance did they leave any record of themselves. A census taken of the poor of Norwich in 1571, extending down to six-year-olds, revealed a surprising number who at seven or eight were attending school; and about the turn of the century a chorister in Bangor cathedral, poor but restless and ambitious, was able to attend several 'country schools' in his native Anglesey where for two shillings or half a crown a quarter he could be coached 'till he had learned accidence' and was qualified to enter Friars School at Bangor. Thence he begged his way to Oxford, and after years of

An Elizabethan schoolroom: diligence

Elizabethan schoolroom: idleness

tutoring in private houses at last sailed into his desired haven of a living in the church under Charles I.

The extent of actual illiteracy in Elizabethan England is hard to gauge; one suspects it was a good deal less prevalent than in early nineteenth-century England, when the old social structure was crumbling under stress of the Industrial Revolution. The fact that respectable folk like churchwardens might sign their names with an 'X' is no indication, for the same person not infrequently uses his name on one document and the symbol on another within a few years or even months. Although laments on the alleged decay of grammar schools and universities were frequent, few expressed concern about the state of primary education, except a handful of advanced educationists, especially such as had experienced in grammar school the sad effects of lack of earlier training (a familiar complaint!). The gentry and merchants who refounded grammar schools which had come to grief during the years of spoliation were rarely moved to take the same steps for chantry schools or singing schools, though to do them justice they often helped any of their household staff who showed promise to enter the grammar school. The chief concern of the state with this grade of society was to see that the children were brought up in industrious and sober habits, and for that the Elizabethan Statute of Artificers, with its apprenticeship code, and the catechising by the parish priest so frequently urged in royal injunctions and episcopal visitations, seemed the proper approach. It was not until 1833 that the state assumed any responsibility for primary education, and not till 1870 that it took the plunge of directly providing it. The Elizabethan state, working on a shoestring budget, was not primarily a provider at all: it was content to see that proper direction was given to those whose moral or legal obligation it was to make the provision.

Schools, like everything else, suffered from the religious

upheavals of the early part of the century. The former cathedral schools soon recovered; those attached to great monasteries like Canterbury and Westminster were refounded by a better distribution of their old endowments. Smaller monastic foundations did not fare so well, but some of them struggled to their feet again with the help of private or municipal benefactions; a lot of these schools had in fact been very small affairs with little educational influence outside their own community. The heaviest casualties were among the chantry schools that taught grammar: some were refounded by local generosity; many vanished for ever. The Speaker of the House of Commons at the opening of the reign reckoned that the country was poorer than it had been by a hundred grammar schools.

The 'lay' foundations of the fourteenth and fifteenth centuries, from Winchester and Eton down to country grammar schools founded by trade gilds or by private citizens or squires, suffered only the temporary set-backs caused by the frequent 'purges' of masters and scholars during successive phases of the Reformation; for of course no school was completely free of clerical jurisdiction. An article which was a hardy annual among the instructions to the bishops and among their enquiries at visitations, was the condition and number of grammar schools in their dioceses—'a matter of no small moment, and chiefly to be looked into by every bishop in his diocese', as the council put it in a letter to Archbishop Grindal in 1580. Here crown and bishops, gentry and merchants were at one. The re-establishment of a sound educational system was at once a guarantee of the religious settlement and the social order (the equivalent indeed of propaganda in the modern state), a contribution towards the economic health and therefore the political independence of the state in these years of stress, and a means of maintaining both the social dignity and the practical competence of the rising generation of gentry. In these circumstances the leeway was soon made up. It has been reckoned that before the end of the reign, through the munificence of merchants, churchmen, gentlemen, even yeomen (the nobility to a less marked degree), England had as many schools as ever. Few corporate towns, Harrison declares, are without at least one,

providing 'sufficient living for a master and usher'. Among the
new foundations are many famous names: Harrow and Rugby,
Uppingham and Repton, Tonbridge and Shrewsbury.

Shrewsbury school became a favourite resort of sons of the
Welsh gentry. Since the early fifteenth century another
border foundation, Oswestry, had been at their service, and a
few ephemeral or dubious foundations in Wales itself are
attributed to the years following the Act of Union; but
Elizabeth's reign added four which have survived: Bangor
(projected under Mary), Ruthin, Carmarthen and Presteigne,
the gifts of a lawyer, a churchman, a peer and a draper. So far
as they went, the Elizabethan grammar schools added their
quota towards fitting Wales into the Tudor social pattern;
but in accordance with the usual time-lag it was the following
century that really established the grammar school system
there, with nine new foundations. In spite of these increasing
local provisions, some of the wealthier and more ambitious
Welsh gentry preferred to send their children to schools in the
heart of England—presumably because in that way they would
be surer of acquiring a good English accent than in schools
where they mixed with their own kind. That was the avowed
reason why Father Augustine Baker was sent to London for his
education at one of the Inns of Court. Sir John Wynn of Gwydir,
the leading gentleman of North Wales and by no means
backward in his support of such measures as the translation of
the Bible and Psalter into Welsh and the publication of Welsh
dictionaries, placed his sons in schools like Eton, Bedford and
St. Albans.

Universities suffered even more heavily than schools from the
troubles of the Reformation; obviously it was harder in such
conspicuous institutions to escape the watchful eye of the bishop
or his commissary. Purges and counter-purges had wrought
havoc in the ranks of fellows and scholars and left deep gashes
in chapels and in libraries, where books of the wrong theological
colour had often been consigned to the flames. Naturally
parents were frightened of sending their young to encounter

these risks. 'Universities do wondrously decay already', Latimer had assured the boy-king, and again, 'It would pity a man's heart to hear that that I hear of the state of Cambridge; what it is in Oxford, I cannot tell.' We can: it was worse, in proportion as the old scholastic theology had been more firmly entrenched there. Once the Elizabethan settlement had given promise of stability, however, both universities soon made up the lost ground and forged still farther ahead. Taking Oxford, still the larger university, as a sample, admissions to the master's degree rose from under seventy at the queen's accession (much the same as in the last reign) to more than twice as many in 1570. The papal bull of that year caused another temporary set-back, and left a permanent mark in the fact that from now on convinced papalists went to one of the foreign seminaries, leaving in the home universities only convinced protestants and the indifferent and time-serving. But undergraduates flocked in as the country became richer, and Harrison, who belonged to both universities, could write of them at the end of the reign in glowing terms that contrast sharply with Latimer's lament of fifty years earlier.

Cambridge had its own troubles, among the chief of which was that puritanism, strong in the East Anglian counties on which it so largely drew, was growing bold enough to challenge the Elizabethan church from the other flank. In 1570 Thomas Cartwright was turned out of the chair of divinity for his presbyterian views, and other expulsions followed. But with a chancellor like Burghley, rootedly pacific, sympathetic with the puritans yet in the queen's confidence, serious disruptions were avoided. It is significant that the two new foundations of the reign, both belonging to its later years, were strongly puritan in tone: Emmanuel became the chief nursing mother to New England, and Sidney Sussex was to give the country Oliver Cromwell. Oxford's only Elizabethan foundation, Jesus, was also characteristic in its way. It was founded in 1571 by Hugh Price, treasurer of St. David's, primarily for the benefit of his fellow-countrymen, who had long frequented other Oxford (and occasionally Cambridge) colleges in considerable numbers. Elizabeth, as befitted a Tudor queen, graciously accepted, or rather appropriated, the rôle of honorary foundress. But the endowment was small, and it took fifty years for the college to make an effective start, after successful appeals to the Welsh gentry and clergy; for they had by then abandoned Glyndŵr's dream of a university, or universities, in Wales itself and accepted the full implications of English citizenship as proclaimed by the Tudors. But not till after one more attempt.

Jesus College, Oxford, founded in 1571: the original Elizabethan 'hall' (on the left) is incorporated in the seventeenth-century buildings

The wealthy and puritanical Sir William Herbert of St. Julians in Monmouthshire planned, while Jesus College was little more than a paper foundation, to devote his estate at Tintern to the purpose, as a remedy for Welsh 'backwardness in religion'; but he died before plans were complete, and his heir, Herbert of Cherbury, thought they could best be fulfilled by bequeathing to Jesus library, years later, his own magnificent library of nine hundred volumes.

The increasing importance of the colleges in the life of the university was among the more striking developments of the century. Rooms were provided in them for undergraduates, instead of only dons, and colleges began to insist on residence in them instead of in scattered lodgings or hostels—a great gain to discipline. Lectures were held there instead of only in the 'schools' provided by the university, and the characteristic tutorial system spread, whether the tutor accompanied the undergraduate from his home, as with the better-off, or was provided, at a fee, by the college. All this naturally increased the cost of residence. At an Oxford college, towards the end of the century, a superior room cost a pound a year, a smaller one ten shillings; how it was furnished depended on the occupant, who provided his own tables, chairs, hangings, rushes, sometimes even window glass, as well as table ware and bed linen. If, as now sometimes happened, he aspired to the luxury of a fire in his room, he must find his own fuel. But very frequently these expenses were reduced to a third or a quarter by the sharing of rooms. The total cost of living 'in a very good sort' at Cambridge some dozen years later was reckoned at £20 a year, perhaps a fifteenth of what a parent with the same money income would have to pay to send his son there today. There does not seem to be much substance in the complaints made by both Latimer under Edward VI and by Harrison in the high Elizabethan period that 'there be none now but great men's sons in colleges', or that 'the most part' were 'either gentlemen or rich men's sons' who brought the university into 'slander' by their idle and luxurious living. Certainly there were more gentlemen and even noblemen than there used to be,

Emmanuel College, Cambridge, founded in 1584

and one reason is clearly put in an imaginary dialogue written early in the century, in which the familiar jeer at learning as an unbecoming and unremunerative pursuit for a gentleman is answered: 'Let me suppose that any foreigner and stranger to our language . . . should come on a mission to our king, and it were necessary for someone to give a reply . . ., the learned children of your ploughman would be selected for the honourable office and exalted far above your hunters and hawkers.'

The argument went home, and of course the increasing influx from a class unused to plain living and high thinking did begin to change the tone of university life. But both the chancellors, Leicester at Oxford and Burghley at Cambridge, neither of them exemplars of frugality in their home lives, set their faces against undergraduate extravagance. Luxury in dress was as firmly put down by university statutes as by civic ordinances, and rules against unlawful games, haunting of taverns and other incitements to idleness multiplied; with what effects it would be rash to judge. Food was certainly not extravagant for the rank and file of undergraduates. Five shillings a week were reckoned enough at Cambridge for meals for a well-to-do knight's son, whereas at this social level, as we have seen earlier, a single modest meal in private quarters cost from five to ten shillings; on the other hand it suggests more generous fare than that of the lawyer at his Inn, where the 'ordinary' generally cost threepence. At Oxford, a little earlier, an allowance of threepence had to cover both dinner and supper for a senior fellow, with bread and beer thrown in; bachelors and undergraduates had to make do on twopence-halfpenny.

Dinner at the scholar's table in an Oxford college is described by a contemporary as 'boiled beef with pottage, bread and beer' (a halfpennyworth of the latter) 'and no more', except what extra 'tuck' the undergraduate might lay in for feast days. Breakfast was not generally allowed for: you found that for yourself, if you could afford it. Those of the highest rank fed more sumptuously at a separate table, and it was always easier for them to obtain 'graces' exempting them from the more irksome conditions for a degree. Still, that did not prevent the poor man from coming up and contriving to make good. There were more matriculants describing themselves as *pleb. fil.* (commoners' sons) than as sons of knights, clergy or gentry, and something like ten per cent put themselves down as 'poor', the lowest grade of all. As we have seen, even the begging scholar was not yet quite an extinct breed.

Country grammar schools had not as yet caught up with Oxford and Cambridge, and become fully residential. Pupils, other than day pupils, lodged in the town, at about two shillings a week (including laundry), though they often fed at the school. The fare of a day-boarder at a private school for children of well-to-do merchants, to judge from a single indication, differed little from that of the ordinary undergraduate, save for the provision of a breakfast of bread-and-butter and fruit, rather more milk and vegetables, and a somewhat more liberal supper, with butcher's meat, eggs and salads.

The curriculum, in school and college alike, was still formally based on the scheme inherited from the educational practice of the Roman Empire: the *trivium* of grammar, logic and rhetoric and the *quadrivium* of arithmetic, geometry, astronomy and music. Grammar of course meant Latin grammar, the key to all other studies since it was the medium of instruction and the international language of learning. Greek, although it had now been taught for two or three generations, still had something of the status of a newcomer, not universally welcomed. But in other respects the New Learning and the Reformation between them were bringing about many readjustments in the traditional scheme of things. Probably the most important was the printed word: lectures need no longer be literally 'readings' now that the student could read his texts

A printing shop, c.1581

103

The redoubtable Dr Dee, 1527–1608

for himself, often in editions from his own university press. A growing sensitiveness to style added importance to rhetoric: Latin was still a flexible living language, and an imaginative teacher could use his teaching of it both to develop literary taste and to stimulate current interests. On the other hand, the close association of logic with theology in the medieval scheme called for a new approach, often a stormy one, to this branch of the *trivium*, and the enthronement of the English Bible as the *vade mecum* of divinity brought in a new text book. Even mathematics had had important theological bearings, and in consequence shared in the general shift of emphasis; for a time it lost much of its academic status, in school and university alike, and developed rather as a 'practical' subject or a private hobby, outside the normal curriculum. The practical needs were chiefly those of the business man and the navigator; as a hobby it was pursued by the numerous dabblers in astrology. In both aspects the redoubtable Dr. Dee, the queen's Welsh astrologer, counted for more than academic lectures. Robert Recorde, a fellow-Welshman who taught at both universities, introduced outside readers to the Arabic sciences of algebra and arithmetic in text books which had an enormous vogue for a century and more after his death in 1558.

From Recorde's Whetstone of Wit

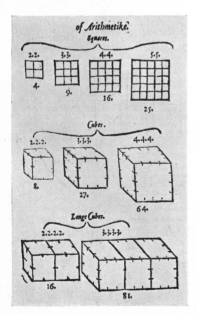

104

Astronomy suffered with mathematics; the telescope lay in the future, and what was taught was an antiquated survival, unaffected by the new theories of Copernicus. It is characteristic that Sir John Davies's fine poem *Orchestra*, published in 1596, describes the universe on orthodox medieval lines and dismisses the Copernican system in an aside. It need hardly be added that other branches of natural science remained untaught for many a long day; but the breeding of stock, and especially of horses and dogs, gave some approach to zoology and the universal interest in gardens to botany. The one great English contribution to contemporary science, the discovery of William Gilbert, the queen's physician, that the earth is a magnet, was published only in the very last year of the century. A more surprising weakness, in so musical an age, is in the teaching of music itself; but the madrigals and the music for lute or virginals which Elizabethans enjoyed at home bore little relationship to the highly mathematical music of the *quadrivium*, which had been studied chiefly as an approach to the intricate modes of medieval church music. These too were out of favour, so much so that organs and choirs themselves had all but been swept away in the general stampede from 'popery' in Edward VI's reign,

Title page of a book on geography

William Camden, 1551–1623: herald, antiquary, historian, topographer; headmaster of Westminster school

and were still frowned on in many quarters. What was left or salvaged of church music was taught by church choirmasters, and secular music was learnt, as always, in the home.

'Modern' subjects fared little better. We have seen something of the provision for modern languages in private schools or by private tuition. Ancient history you read in your Latin or Greek authors; for modern history you depended on the chronicles which were to be found in every gentleman's library. Similarly with geography: apart from the outdated stuff included in astronomy, it could be picked up from the many books of travel issuing from the press and greedily snapped up, notably Hakluyt's immortal collection, which appeared soon after the Armada; and it is hard to believe that Camden's pupils at Westminster were left in ignorance of the history and geography of their own land. Sometimes private tuition took the form of an 'extra' provided at the grammar school for those willing to pay: Sir John Wynn's son at Bedford was taught French, Italian and music (vocal and instrumental) as well as Latin, Greek and Hebrew: a formidable programme, if it was taken seriously! Even writing, then a fine art, might be an 'extra' taught by a visiting scrivenor; lack of attention to this accomplishment by the regular masters was then as now a fruitful source of parental complaints. The mercantile community of London provided itself with a good variety of schools to meet its special needs, with a better innings for mathematics than at the universities. Most striking of all is the college endowed by the great Elizabethan merchant and financier Sir Thomas Gresham to provide weekly lectures in all the recognised academic subjects from a frankly 'modern' angle. Before it died of later neglect, Gresham College more than justified itself by the part it played in the movement leading to the foundation of the Royal Society.

The universal Cinderella of studies was the mother tongue. Voices had already been raised, weighty ones too, in favour of English both as a medium of instruction and as a subject worthy of study in itself, but so far educational practice had not responded. English grammar was learned through Latin grammar, English style through translation from Latin, literary criticism through rhetoric. The results were not unimpressive. Much worse was the case of the Welsh pupil, who had no printed Welsh classics to draw on. The language had to be transmitted orally at home, with the aid of a few recently printed primers, grammars and dictionaries; what saved it from extinction, and with it a rich body of inherited culture, was the Welsh Bible.

For schoolboy and undergraduate alike the standard tests of proficiency were the written 'theme' and the oral 'disputation', both, of course, in Latin. Like all other tests they tended to lend themselves to mechanical memorising, but at their best they did encourage some respect for logical thought and even some selective reading for cogent instances, since the theme or the matter for debate might be ancient or contemporary. They bore something of the character of the modern school 'project'. The public open-air inter-school disputations—the contemporary equivalent of debating matches or 'top of the form' contests—which Stow remembered in the London of his youth, were given up because, not surprisingly, they descended into slanging matches and then to 'blows with their satchels full of books', becoming a public nuisance; but in a more domestic way the institution survived. At about sixteen, sometimes earlier, rarely much later, the schoolboy was ready for college. The full Arts course leading to the master's degree took seven years, on the same pattern as the seven-years' apprenticeship to a craft, culminating in the 'masterpiece' of the final disputation; if degrees were sought in theology, medicine or law they had to follow after this. But the habit was growing, especially at Cambridge, of going out of residence at the end of the four-years' 'bachelor' course, returning only for the master's disputation.

The schoolboy had to put up with a ten-hour day, from about seven to five, with only short breaks; the undergraduate, under less constant supervision, no doubt got away with much less than this. Vacations at all stages amounted to the twelve days of Christmas with two to four extra days for good measure, and twelve at Easter; Shrewsbury was exceptional in making a nine-day break at Whitsun. There was no regular weekly holiday or even half-holiday, except Sunday, when relaxation might be allowed outside the compulsory service hours. It was left to Oliver Cromwell to compensate for docking even this by instituting a monthly half-holiday for students and apprentices. But there were alleviations even in school hours. Dramatic talent was encouraged as part of both school and college education, and plays were often acted in public. At St. Albans, a school otherwise in high repute, there were complaints in the next reign that boys acquired in school habits of swearing, tippling and 'drinking tobacco', which do not suggest an unduly cramped life.

To the Elizabethan mind education was neither a public service provided by the state nor a marketable commodity, though commercial habits of mind were giving fuller play to this second aspect; it was rather a work of charity like almshouses and hospitals. Ideally, if Christians all did their duty after their means, school and college were within reach of all, financially and geographically. They very nearly were, for all willing and able to profit by them: far more nearly than they ever became again till our own day. The foundation scholar at school or college had his tuition and 'commons' free, apart from a possible entrance fee, which might be graduated according to rank. He would of course have to meet any extras in the way of either tuition or amenities, as well as his text books: at least a Bible, a Latin grammar and a compendium of manners for school, the texts of his authors for college, with paper, inkhorn, quills, penknife for shaping them (also, less legitimately, for 'scratching out' mistakes); and to hold them all the satchel that accompanied the shining morning face to school. The fee-paying pupil at Bedford cost his father £13 2s. 3d. a year, including board and lodging and all 'extras'; we have already had some samples of what the 'commoner' paid at college. Private tuition with board, under a reputable tutor, would cost much the same as a good school, but at a minor establishment or with a 'scratch' tutor forty shillings a year would meet the bill. Except in the largest schools the staff would consist of the master and one usher; school cleaning was usually done by the children themselves—in school hours, one hopes! Girls often went to

The universal text-book: Lily's Latin Grammar

school at the primary stage, but after that they had to depend on home tuition. The quality of that must have been pretty high, judging by results: upper-class women of the age could have shown a clean pair of heels educationally to any later generation until we reach the opening of the universities to women, and even the squire's or farmer's wife could often write a decent letter. The age of Shakespeare had little to blush for in its educational practice.

Further Reading

The Elizabethan Home (*see* Chapter IV).

L. S. Knight, *Welsh Independent Grammar Schools to 1600*, 1926.

C. E. Malet, *History of the University of Oxford*, Vol. II, 1924.

J. B. Mullinger, *The University of Cambridge*, Vol. II, 1884.

E. M. W. Tillyard, *The Elizabethan World Picture*, 1943.

Foster Watson, *English Grammar Schools to 1660*, 1908.

VII

Arts and Pastimes

The linking of arts with pastimes came more naturally to the Elizabethans than it does to us. They were less solemn, less self-conscious about art than we tend to be. This is no doubt associated with the fact that art had not yet become professionalised. No Elizabethan, or hardly any, got his bread and butter merely by writing or composing or by any of the visual arts. Either he was the pure amateur, the man of means who followed his art as a hobby and circulated his work among his friends, or he made his living as a craftsman or an entertainer, not by his creative work. The architects of the age were paid as master masons; what few painters the country produced were officially engravers or house decorators; musicians lived by providing courtly diversions for royal palace or noble household: dramatists, too, until the public clamoured for a share in these, and Elizabeth in 1574 licensed Burbage and four others to act anywhere 'as well

A royal picnic

for the recreation of our loving subjects as for our solace and pleasure'. This concession was destined to provide a living for William Shakespeare, not as dramatist, but as actor-manager. There is no point at which we can draw a hard-and-fast line between the poem or play, madrigal or portrait which has justified the accident of survival and proved immortal, and the doggerel ballad hawked and sung by Autolycus and his tribe, the interlude cobbled together by Peter Quince and Bully

'*What shall he have that kill'd the deer*

Bottom, or the crude woodcut or inn-sign or 'pretty slight drollery in water work' of the travelling craftsman; nor, for that matter between any of these and the village 'maying' which might draw on any or all of these arts. It was the most natural thing in the world to build a theatre next to a bear garden, maybe with the same owner. The beginnings of serious literary and musical criticism, with a Sidney or a Dowland, towards the end of the century, mark the end of this phase and the dawn of the more sophisticated, classical and scientific age of the Stuarts.

The form of recreation remotest from creative art was the universally popular sport of hunting. It was the sport of kings, queens and nobles, with their own deer parks; outlaws where the deer still ran wild, or poachers (the youthful Shakespeare among them) who laughed at boundary fences, might indulge their appetite for free venison at their peril. Hawking was even more exclusive, for it was easier to keep your hawks to yourself than your deer park. These were courtly accomplishments, learned in a gentleman's household; some old-fashioned aristocrats still found them more fitting to their 'degree' than beggarly book-learning. But hawking at least was not beyond the reach of wealthy London citizens, who (says Stow) 'do rather want

111

'Faulconrie'

leisure than goodwill' to indulge in it more freely than they do. On the other hand, coursing hares and rabbits was a sport open to everyone, and in the country everyone joined in. Hunting the fox was not yet a sport, but a public duty, discharged with the help of bow and arrow or of gun, and often rewarded by premiums from parish funds. In this respect the age was humaner than ours; but in the addiction to bear-baiting and bull-baiting we see another expression of the taste which made it necessary for the dramatist to litter his stage with corpses and to include among stage properties items like '3 violls of blood and a sheep's gather' (i.e. entrails). Elizabeth had had her own bears and bear-ward since she was six; as queen she found them useful for keeping foreign ambassadors happy. Nor was any pity wasted on the wretched bedraggled and muzzled bears dragged around the country by their bear-wards to earn them a few coppers by dancing on the village green, in market squares or inn yards. How this private supply was kept up in the conditions that prevailed here remains something of a mystery; but kept up it was. Years later, when Caernarvon castle surrendered to the Roundheads in 1646, a formal document was drawn up giving free quarter to a Lancashire bear-ward and his 'great bear' brought in to beguile the tedium of the siege.

Football, as then played, was marked by the same love of violence and the chase. With few rules, unlimited teams, no

'Shall we go and kill us venison?'

line, no 'gate', and a minimum of penalised fouls, whole villages or districts challenged each other, and there were few matches that did not bring their toll of casualties, from broken heads to broken necks. George Owen of Henllys has left us a full and vivid description of a variety known in his native Pembrokeshire as *knappan*. This was a Welsh form of a familiar English

112

word meaning 'to knock', though the learned and patriotic Owen, who had often played the game and still carried the 'signes and seales' of it in his 'heade handes and other partes', would have traced both *knappan* and the 'hurling' played by

Bull- and bear-rings

'our ancient cozens the Cornishmen' back to Brutus the Trojan, ancestor of the Britons; and he thought he recognised it in a game described in Virgil's *Aeneid*. It was played with a wooden ball of box, yew, crabtree or holly, just big enough to hold in the hand, 'boyled in tallow for to make it slipperye', by players stripped to the waist and with hair and beards prudently kept short for the occasion. Most of the players played on foot, and barefoot at that, but some on horseback, polo fashion, with cudgels three and a half feet long, the object being to plant the ball in one's own village. The field might extend for several miles, the players (if Owen is to be credited) to as many as two thousand. Certain villages by ancient custom challenged their traditional rivals on set days: Shrove Tuesday, Easter Monday, Low Sunday, Ascension Day and Corpus Christi; and on these occasions 'there would alsoe resorte to the place diverse victualers with meate, drinke and wyne of all sortes, alsoe merchauntes, mercers, and pedlers would provide stalls, and boothes, to shewe and utter theire wares', while the players hurled defiance or encouragement at each other in Welsh. Gentry and yokels played together as at any village cricket match. Owen, like some retired colonel writing to *The Times*, laments the way the game has gone down through the neglect of ancient rules and the intrusion of personal feuds; nevertheless he quotes with pride the comment of a stranger who happened on this struggling mass of humanity in the year 1588, and on being told it was all in play commented, 'If this be but playe, I cold wishe the spaniardes were here to see our plaies in England. Certes they would be in bodielye feare of our warre.'

The government took a different view. Football was too frequent a cause of riot and bloodshed and too great a distraction from archery practice, the contemporary equivalent of Home Guard drill. Tennis, played in indoor courts in gentlemen's houses spacious enough to provide the amenity, was another matter: Henry VIII, we remember, was a very skilful player. But football was frowned on by others besides the guardians of law and order: merchants disliked it because it so often meant lost working days; gospellers and puritans because if working days were not used it was played on Sundays. On the other hand Mulcaster, the most advanced educationist of his day, was a firm champion of football, but he wanted to reduce the game to some sort of order by introducing coaches and referees. Yeomen and peasants, and townsmen too, were for their part ready enough to carry out their archery practice; it had the sanction of long tradition, reminding them how in their grandfather's days it was by superior bowmanship that the English, not to mention the Welsh, had made the Frenchmen run. But football let off far more steam, and even country gentry, if they had not yet acquired courtly polish, were reluctant as magistrates to put it down, orders from London notwithstanding.

In a less boisterous way, music and dancing were diversions in which all classes shared: not, as a rule, together (though that might often happen at village festivals or at the squire's wedding), but in their several ways. The May-day dancing on the village green, or the many local varieties of morris-dance that marked the chief local festivals, need not detain us; but the ubiquitous fiddler, at these and many other popular functions, reminds us how very common was the ability to play a musical instrument, in some sort or other. A good fiddler, fit to be engaged at the theatre, could command as much as £1 for two hours' playing: about a month's wages for an ordinary labourer, and enough to provide an Oxford undergraduate with a good room for the whole academic year. Many towns had their paid bands of waits to play in the street on appropriate occasions. The upper-class equivalent was the small orchestra which played at meals in the minstrels'

Alfresco music

gallery and gave more elaborate performances on special occasions. The royal court and the royal chapel were famous for their music, and had been since Henry VI's day; even the careful Henry VII did not cut down on this item of expenditure, nor did his granddaughter, who could in other matters be parsimonious to a fault. William Byrd, although for at least part of his adult life he was an avowed catholic recusant, became organist of her Chapel Royal in 1569, and six years later he was granted a joint monopoly with his old master Tallis (remembered today by the well-known 'canon' still often sung in church) of the sale of printed music, for which he imported his type from Nuremberg. Byrd was one of our great composers of both sacred and secular music, and he helped to introduce the country to the latest Italian styles, making music yet another field of Italian influence on English culture of the age.

The doubts whether church music would go by the board with the rest of Mary's religious restorations when her half-sister succeeded were soon put to rest. In the very first year of her reign Elizabeth ordered that choristers should be paid their customary fees and that 'it be permitted at the beginning of prayers . . . to sing a hymn or such like song, in the best melody or music, as long as the words be distinguishable'. By the end of the reign the position of music in church was secure, though it was a much simplified music, and to make the words 'distinguishable' the psalms were sung in the Sternhold and Hopkins metrical version ('Geneva jigs' to popish ears) of which the Old Hundredth has remained a favourite. Some editions even included English metrical versions, set to music, of the Lord's Prayer, the Ten Commandments, many of the canticles and early hymns of the church, the Nicene Creed and—a real *tour de force*—the Athanasian Creed. Gradually, however, the more sophisticated church music sponsored by Byrd at the Chapel Royal won its way back into cathedrals until the puritan attacks of the next century.

In the ordinary parish church, with an untrained choir (if any) and a few amateur instrumentalists to lead the singing, music depended on the congregation, and Sternhold and Hopkins's Psalms 'with apt notes to sing them withall' helped them out, in some editions, by adding to the melody the alto, tenor and bass parts. This both reflected and helped to diffuse a popular delight in part singing. 'Faire songes at fouer partes' were becoming a part of the normal equipment of any gentle or middle-class household, whether the printed volumes of madrigals (the popular musical form imported from Italy but soon adapted to English idiom), of which some forty collections were published during the generation after 1590, or manuscript 'bookes of musicke' copied by the singers themselves. 'Manual labourers and mechanical artificers of all sorts', declared the author of *Praise of Musicke* in 1588, 'keepe such a chaunting and singing in their shoppes, the tailor on his bulk, the shoemaker at his last, the mason at his wall, the shipboy at his oar, and the tiler on the housetop'; almost the words in which Erasmus, over sixty years earlier, had urged that the scriptures should made familiar to all be in their own tongue—except that it was not always the words of Holy Writ that these 'mechanical artificers' were 'chaunting'! If we may believe Thomas Morley, who wrote a *Plaine and Easie Introduction to Practicall Musicke* in 1597, the casual guest invited after supper to join the

A singing exercise

customary family sing-song was met with flat incredulity if he
disclaimed an ear for music: 'Yea, some whispered to others,
demanding how I was brought up.' Certainly a gentleman
with any social ambitions would see that his children were
'brought up' to sing and play: had not Henry VIII himself
set the example? It is a constant refrain in the many enquiries
of Sir John Wynn about suitable schools for turning his country-
bred sons into good men of the world. We have seen how
highly Sir Christopher Hatton's music at Eltham was esteemed;
and Drake himself, when he wished to impress the world with
the majesty of England, saw to it that the *Golden Hind* carried
a small but good orchestra.

To be able to sing solos to the lute, or to play them on the
virginals, was also a valued and widespread accomplishment.
In this same year 1597 John Dowland, a university graduate
in music who had travelled widely and became a court lutenist,
published his *First Booke of Songes or Ayres*, which ran into
four editions and was the first of many issued by himself and
other accomplished musicians. Dowland became a best-seller
because (as Fuller puts it) he 'compounded English with
foreign skill' like the best architects of the day; for he based his
melodies on embellished popular folk song, the 'carol' that had
such a vogue in the fifteenth century, and he added lute accom-
paniments which introduced the amateur player to new musical
ideas from abroad, setting them to poems which were also
works of art in their own right.

Poetry and music thus lived in close association. If fewer could
write poems than play the lute or join in a madrigal or catch,
the urge to write it was astonishingly widespread, and the
poems that have survived, sometimes by the mere accident
of preservation with the accompanying tune, are only a fraction
of what were written. At the very lowest there were the writers,
hawkers and singers of street ballads, by whose means the
man in the street had his ear attuned to simple rhymes and
rhythms; this made him the readier to accept plays written in
verse than a generation brought up on the snappy prose of the

117

daily press, and so helped to link poetry with drama too. At the same time themes from classical and foreign literature began to seep through even to popular doggerel, providing a new repertory of the gory, martial or sentimental detail in demand, and preparing the public to appreciate a drama incorporating these new departures, if it were only on the level of the 'tedious brief scene of young Pyramus and his love Thisbe; very tragical mirth'.

All this helps to explain the outburst, during the last two decades of the queen's reign, of a drama which was in the fullest sense popular and yet in close touch with the wider cultural currents of the age. 'Of late time', says Stow, writing in 1598 of the traditional diversions of the Londoner, 'in place of these stage plays hath been used comedies, tragedies, interludes, and histories, both true and feigned.' The 'stage plays' to which he refers are the mysteries and moralities so popular in all the great towns, and many of the smaller ones, in the later middle ages, but now worn threadbare. The new impulse naturally came from the quarters best able to afford it: the royal court and the lordly mansion. In both the entertainer, were he minstrel, clown or 'tumbler', had always been part of the regular establishment. When once wider reading and travel had developed the taste for new dramatic forms and new scenic devices, it was not a long step to combine the accustomed music and its accompanying verse with the pageantry and the buffoonery into a new type of dramatic performance, and to search for dramatic talent either on the spot or from outside. On the one hand there was the masque, complete with music, elaborate *décor*, declamation and tableaux, performed as a rule by princely or noble amateurs for their own and each other's entertainment; on the other the entertainment provided for their patrons and paymasters by bands of players hired for the occasion or under regular patronage: the choristers of the Chapel Royal and St. Paul's school, for example, who performed before the court, or the bands of itinerant actors (sometimes municipal troupes analagous to the town waits), to whom some of the nobility had since Henry VIII's day been according their patronage.

The impetus extended far beyond the halls of the mighty. Other schools, as we have seen, found in current educational theory good warrant for putting up their own plays, not without hope that some day they too might be called upon to perform before the queen or one of her magnates. Inns of court and universities did likewise, and the stage-struck undergraduate was already a familiar spectacle. Finally bands of local amateurs, catching the fever and scenting *largesse* from afar, began to proffer their services on public occasions, hoping like Quince and his band to get past the obstructions of some officious Philostrate. By these means the itinerant

Orchestra and masquers

actor began to emerge from the company of the juggler, the minstrel and the clown, and the diversions of court and nobility to filter through to the general public. Plenty of boys had enough stage experience to undertake the female parts which public feeling would not yet allow women to play. Costume was as varied and lavish as on the medieval stage; scenery, too, at least in the masque, which could draw on the resources of royal palace or ducal mansion.

This raised new problems. First the problem of that disreputable figure the actor. A government bent on putting down vagabondage could not be expected to welcome with open arms the rise of a new race of vagabonds. A similar dilemma was presented by the Welsh bards, recognised from time immemorial as purveyors and guardians of the language in its classic form, which was taught nowhere else, as well as arbiters of gentility. Bards had been part of the normal staff of a Welsh princely court, and afterwards of a gentleman's household: so far all was well, so long as the gentry continued to support them. But there were also wandering bards who went from house to house picking up what entertainment and *largesse* they could by singing the praises of the host and his ancestry.

How were they to be distinguished from the mere tramp or charlatan, unless someone vouched for them? The queen accordingly in 1568 commissioned a number of Welsh gentlemen to summon an *eisteddfod* of recognised bards to test the capacities of pretenders to the title, the last to be held before the national revival of the late eighteenth century. This, however, only safeguarded standards at the top; the wandering charlatan remained at large until an Act of four years later left him, after an unsuccessful attempt to exempt the 'minstrels of Wales', to the tender mercies of the vagrancy laws in company with other 'minstrells, bear-wards, pedlars, etc.'—a comprehensive etcetera which also left the roving actor open to arrest unless he could show a magistrate's license.

The bard and the free-lance actor were thus in the same boat; but both were safe in the household or under the guarantee of a man of quality. Luckily, the most powerful peer of the realm till his death in 1588, the earl of Leicester, redeemed many sad political, military and personal deficiencies by a genuine concern for learning and the arts. This he showed both in his chancellorship of Oxford and in his patronage of James Burbage's company of actors, one of the four to which the queen in 1574, two years after the Vagrancy Act, issued her general license to act throughout the kingdom. More luckily still, the queen herself loved plays, and already had her own company of actors. Companies multiplied, and when one patron died another took over his actors. There were half a dozen companies with London headquarters before the Armada, and their competition for actors, for playwrights and for the public was a healthy stimulus to the drama.

There remained, however, the problems of the playhouse and the play itself. Traditional makeshifts no longer sufficed; besides, performances were becoming expensive, and the playgoer must be prepared to pay for his fun, which meant shutting out the non-payer. For a time the courtyards of large inns, with their tiers of galleries, offered a solution. The practice was relatively new when Elizabeth became queen, but within a decade or two of her accession half a dozen inns in London— naturally the actors' favourite resort, since the largest audiences could be assembled there—were laying themselves out for such performances. This raised new difficulties for the civic authorities: the city was already congested enough in all conscience without these jostling crowds besieging the inns, provoking all manner of disorders, increasing the danger of plague, and inciting the workmen and apprentices to idleness (for all performances were matinées); and behind all these perfectly sound objections lay the deep-seated puritan prejudice against 'mummery' of any sort. The actors' patrons, usually backed by the privy council, on which

The Swan Theatre, built c. *1593*

they were sure of a spokesman, were too powerful to be defied by the city; but by means of licenses it was able to impose its authority on the choice of play and the place of acting. Too much of the profit, moreover, went to the innkeepers, who charged the wealthier clients for their places in the galleries, leaving the actors to make do with what could be collected from the groundlings in the yard. Accordingly in 1576 Burbage borrowed money to build a permanent theatre, holding something like a thousand spectators, outside the city limits—an eloquent tribute to the popularity of the drama. Burbage did not succeed in making it pay, but it soon found imitators: four others, of still greater capacity, were built before the end of the century. The dominance of the London theatre was established, though its seat of authority was not yet the West End, but the South Bank; and through the tours of the great companies, and their discovery of acting talent up and down the land, their standards were gradually imposed on the country at large. It is believed, for example, that in 1587 a visit of the Queen's Players to Stratford, one of the regular ports of call for both this company and the earl of Worcester's, decided young William Shakespeare, at a critical stage in the family fortunes, to quit his tutoring in country houses (if that was indeed how he had been employed up to now) and to try his luck on the London stage.

This proved a decisive step towards the solution of the other problem, that of the play. Noble patrons acquainted with continental and classical standards naturally looked for more than hack writers on hackneyed themes. About a decade after the first theatre was built they started employing men of university standing and literary gifts to write their plays. From the swollen population of the Elizabethan university there were plenty of bright young men to choose from, men who had become stage-struck in their undergraduate days and from lack of inclination or lack of chance had never settled down to steady employment, but drifted to London to pick up a precarious living in the Elizabethan equivalent of Grub Street. Among these educated penny-a-liners who supplied plays for the theatre during the years immediately before and after the Armada were a few men of genius—notably Marlowe— capable of bringing to the drama high poetry, infectious zest and wide knowledge: everything but the discipline so conspicuously lacking in their private lives. All were dead by 1593, most of them very young, two at least dying violent deaths, several under suspicion of blasphemy, atheism and the wildest

The Globe Theatre, Southwark

deeds. There followed a widespread outbreak of plague which closed the London theatres and sent the companies on tour. Such manifestations of divine judgement were too plain to be missed by the enemies of the playhouse.

It is at this point that Shakespeare arrives. He had already been employed in touching up plays for his company, and had just written for them his first original play, *Love's Labour's Lost*. Soon his chronicle plays brought him to the pinnacle of fame, and before the end of the reign many of his greatest comedies, tragedies and poems had appeared, and he had become part-owner of the Globe. The future of English drama was assured. It has been calculated that by 1595 the London theatres were between them attracting weekly audiences of some fifteen thousand, at a penny, twopence or threepence apiece, with takings from each performance not far short of the ten pounds the company would have earned by an appearance at court. And the actor is no longer just a disreputable vagabond. Edward Alleyne, a player of tragic parts in the same company with Shakespeare and partner with his wealthy self-made father-in-law Henslowe in the ownership of theatres and bear gardens, endows a college in his native Dulwich and writes to the 'good sweet mouse' his wife, while on tour during the plague year of 1593, like any country gentleman, with advice about the right time for sowing spinach and parsley and the avoidance of infection. Shakespeare himself retires to Stratford as a highly respected burgess for the last five years of his life.

Another new profession, that of architect, can also trace its origins to Elizabeth's reign. It is true that great builders like Burghley or Bess of Hardwick insisted on their own designs, and treated the master mason they employed as no more than a craftsman responsible for seeing that the workmen conformed with it: a sort of clerk of the works at most. But in the career of Robert Smythson, beginning as mere 'freemason', ending, in 1614 (on the witness of his mural tablet in Wollaton church) as 'architector', and founding a dynasty of architects, we can trace the increasing share of the master craftsman in the

A self-portrait by Nicholas Hilliard, 1537–1619

overall planning of great houses like Longleat, Hardwick or the Middle Temple, in all of which he had a hand. Landscape gardening, too, was developing into a fine art planned in close association with the house itself. But here the native artist, however successfully he may have blended foreign fashion with native tradition, did not like the playwright stand in the van of advance, but rather worshipped from afar his Italian or Flemish masters. Even more was this true of painting, which apart from the still primitive 'water work' on the walls of churches and houses was confined to a few portraits by native artists limping a long way after their acknowledged master Holbein, whom More had brought here in Henry VIII's day. Not until Nicholas Hilliard, the Devonshire goldsmith, was employed by the queen for tasks like engraving her great seal, was a new native tradition in portrait painting established; for Hilliard taught himself at a very early age the art of miniature painting, basing his work more on the medieval missals he had seen at home than on the portraiture of Holbein, to whom as in duty bound he professed allegiance. Soon he was selling the queen's portrait in miniature to obsequious courtiers for enormous sums like 'forty, fifty or a hundred ducats apiece' (perhaps as much as £40) and then executing for them miniatures of themselves or their friends. A new and long characteristic school of English painting had been born.

Further Reading

J. Q. Adams, *Shakespearian Playhouses* (illustrated).

G. B. Harrison, *Shakespeare's Fellows*, 1923.

M. Marples, *A History of Football* (illustrated), 1954.

J. Lees-Milne, *Tudor Renaissance* (*see* Chapter IV).

B. Pattison, *Music and Poetry of the English Renaissance*, 1948.

VIII

The Poor

One of the major achievements of the age of Elizabeth was its handling of the problem of the Poor. 'The Poor' did not mean just what we would call the under-privileged. That sort of poor, men had been taught, would be always with them. The magnificent and often-quoted speech of Ulysses in *Troilus and Cressida* expresses as no other words can the spirit of the age and its deep-rooted conviction: human society, like the heavenly bodies, must 'observe degree, priority and place'.

> *Take but degree away, untune that string,*
> *And, hark, what discord follows! . . .*
> *Then everything includes itself in power,*
> *Power into will, will into appetite.*

To each degree there was an appropriate way of living, some of necessity less comfortable than others, inasmuch as some carried less heavy responsibilities and 'charges'. Failing this,

> *the bounded waters*
> *Should lift their bosoms higher than the shores,*
> *And make a sop of all this solid globe.*

It has been estimated that in Elizabethan Exeter 'grinding poverty was the lot of more than half the population'; but this was not the sort of thing that disturbed the public conscience. So much depends on what you are led to expect of life, and very few of these unfortunates ever imagined, for themselves, any other way of life. For the few who did, the age left many doors unbolted, but it did not deliberately throw them open, or there would have followed that unseemly scramble that turned appetite into 'an universal wolf' driven in the end to 'eat up himself'. Those hardy spirits who ventured beyond their 'degree' must expect no pity if they failed to make the grade. On the other hand Christian charity imposed the duty of easing the lot of the less fortunate at special seasons, or when poverty pressed harder than usual: in old age, say, or in time of famine, pestilence or drought; and we shall see that the Elizabethans were in no way behind their forefathers—rather the contrary— in responding to this call.

The challenge that worried and even terrified responsible men of the Elizabethan age was that of the men and women with- out any visible or legitimate means of subsistence at all. The inflated numbers of these derelicts and ne'er-do-wells under- mined the whole conception of 'degree' as Shakespeare puts it into the mouth of Ulysses, or, more prosaically, as that teen- age wiseacre Edward VI put it in a sort of sixth-form essay on the state of the commonwealth. 'As in the body', he says, 'no part hath too much, nor too little, so in a Common-Wealth ought not every part to have *ad victum et non ad saturitatem.*' 'For maintenance, not excess'; and maintenance was not just a matter of calories but a whole way of life: excess at one social level might be the bare minimum for sustaining another. 'And there is no Part admitted to the Body', he goes on, 'that doth not work and take pains, so there ought to be no part of the Common-wealth to be but laboursome in his Voca- tion. The Gentleman ought to labour in Service in his Country; the Servingman ought to wait diligently on his master; the Artificer ought to labour in his Work; the Husbandman in Tilling the Ground; the Merchant in passing the Tempests; but the Vagabonds ought clearly to be banished, as is the superfluous Humour of the Body.' It was certainly a formidable problem. Harrison, no pessimist, reckoned the number of vagabonds at ten thousand. This gives something like one in five hundred of the population. But Harrison did not write when things were at their worst; besides, it was mainly an urban problem, and to arrive at a true picture of the proportions of the plague we should have to compare his estimate with the total urban population, which would be mere guess-work. The city of Norwich, an exceptionally advanced and enlightened community, reckoned in 1570 that there were more than two thousand beggars in the city, which must have meant over ten per cent of the population.

Almsgiving

The menace was more than a century old when the Tudors came in, but it was only under them that the state of the country afforded the necessary breathing space from war and pestilence to allow of serious investigation and reflection. Never before, and never again till the late eighteenth century, was there such a deluge of literature on the subject. Manuscripts were circulated among friends, and many of them eventually printed, like the singularly able *Discourse of the Common Weal* written under Edward VI but published anonymously under Elizabeth. Enlightened municipalities sent in careful and detailed reports to the privy council. Preachers made it the theme of many a sermon, with a concreteness and topicality rarely to be found among their medieval counterparts the preaching friars. Finally there were frequent discussions in parliament, rising in a grand crescendo to the full dress debate on the state of the nation in 1597, which issued in a Poor Law so comprehensive in its scope that it remained almost intact till 1834 and has only been finally superseded in our own day.

Naturally there was much fumbling before this result was reached. What exactly had gone wrong, and who was to blame (for someone must be)? Was it greedy landlords, causing rural depopulation by enclosure and rack-renting? Or royal debasers of the currency, making everyone's shilling worth less? Or unscrupulous merchants pandering to the taste for foreign luxuries instead of finding markets for our own industries and importing only what these needed to keep them going? Or the decay of charity? Or just a double dose of original sin in the work-shy labourer? Some gave one answer, some another; many of the causes alleged by contemporaries, and for that matter by later historians, were rather effects or symptoms or short-term remedies that ended by making matters

The Elizabethan Underworld

worse. The roots lie in the break-up of feudal society in the fourteenth century, culminating in the general confusion of the Wars of the Roses. The new society was shaping itself under the Tudors, but anti-social habits, as the 'depressed areas' learned to their cost during our own inter-war period, are more quickly learned than dropped, and the victims of the long-drawn crisis did not readily fit themselves into the new pattern. Nor was recovery helped by the rapid reversals of fortune which resulted from inflation, the fruit of American gold and successive debasements of the coinage. The end product was seen in what a contemporary pamphleteer picturesquely calls 'the rowsy ragged rabblement of rakehells' who infested the roads in great bands till the very dogs barked (as our nursery rhyme still reminds us) when the beggars were coming to town.

Contemporary verse, drama and satire, as well as the whole gamut of descriptive and controversial pamphlets, combine to introduce us to the different layers of these dregs of Elizabethan society. They had their recently-invented canting slang, and each grade had its own cant name: Harrison enumerates twenty-three varieties, fourteen male and nine female. In modern terms they included the city slicker and the confidence trickster, the violent gangster and the whining imposter who can sham any sort of illness or disablement; and with them all, and always liable to be infected by their company, decent fellows looking for a job and those who had always preferred the life of the road: jugglers, clowns, bear-wards, minstrels, actors. For the whole problem was complicated by the fact that to the sickness of a dying social order were added the birthpangs of a new. The most conspicuous of these was involuntary unemployment, a novel phenomenon arising from the pressure on local crafts, serving local needs, to adapt themselves to the demands of a fluctuating world market, liable to interruption by obscure events abroad. Even at the end of the Napoleonic wars statesmen were mystified by it, and just how near are we to understanding it today? No wonder Tudor statesmen fumbled. We do not usually go to Shakespeare for lessons in economics, but in *Henry the Eighth* he describes in the person of Norfolk the impact of unemployment, with the familiar gloss of high taxation, in his own grandfather's day:

> *The clothiers all, not able to maintain*
> *The many to them longing, have put off*
> *The spinsters, carders, fullers, weavers, who,*
> *Unfit for other life, compell'd by hunger,*
> *And lack of other means, in desperate manner,*
> *Daring the event to the teeth, are all in uproar—*

just the sort of uproar a government with no police force and no army had most reason to dread.

From the government's point of view, then, it was primarily a question of law and order, and pre-Elizabethan remedies were mainly of a hand-to-mouth or a punitive character. Measures were taken to prevent actual famine by keeping a hand on the corn market; Wolsey's answer to the clothiers who 'put off' the workmen dependent on them because the cloth would not sell was to order the merchants to buy it willy-nilly; for involuntary unemployment was still assumed to be a passing phase, due perhaps to the 'wilfulness' of employers no less than voluntary unemployment was to the wilfulness of workpeople. To deal with vagrancy, Acts of increasing ferocity laid down penalties culminating in the savage law of 1547 which condemned the persistent vagabond to slavery and in the last resort death. Immediate responsibility rested on the local authorities; the state's concern was to see that they did their job and to deal with the vagrant of no fixed abode, who must somehow be pinned down to a parish. But it was recognised on all hands that such measures did not go to the root of the matter, and

Whipping a vagabond

The stocks

that a long-term solution could only lie in what had been extolled in the middle ages as the cardinal virtue of Christian charity, or what the humanistic eighteenth century called by the colder name of philanthropy.

Unhappily, the institutions created by medieval charity had also suffered grievously in the social upheaval of the later middle ages. Monastic charity had shrunk to something like two to three per cent of monastic income, and was largely frittered away in indiscriminate alms; even the great 'hospitals' or hospices for travellers, for the sick and infirm, for orphans and the destitute, had fallen into decrepitude by the early fifteenth century; and it appears from samples taken that hardly more than a quarter of them were doing a useful job when Henry VIII secularised their revenues with those of the monasteries. The urgent need for stimulating charity to meet this challenge was what inspired many of the great preachers of the age. They had learned other things from their Bibles besides patriotic fervour against the enemies of the Lord from without: the Hebrew prophets and the parables of the New Testament inspired them to bitter denunciations of His enemies within who were sapping the foundations of the social and moral order, along with practical exhortations to conduct more worthy a Christian society. Few had the fiery but homely eloquence of a Latimer, but his Elizabethan successors used the pulpit with the same telling effect as a forum for the social conscience, and between them they must have reached as wide a section of the public as the daily press of today.

Elizabeth had the advantage of much valuable experience gained by some of the more populous towns in grappling with their own problems. London naturally set the tone. The city was fortunate in having been granted by the crown four secularised medieval 'hospitals' and a disused royal palace, in which appropriate methods of dealing with different categories of 'poor' could be tried out under the wise guidance of the bishop, Nicholas Ridley, who had great influence with Edward VI. St. Bartholomew's was appropriated to the sick poor, and provided with a hundred beds (as compared with forty in the middle ages), one physician and three surgeons. That these were

The courtyard of Leycester's Hospital, Warwick
The medieval Hall of the United Guilds was, in 1571, converted by the Earl of Leicester into a hospital for twelve aged blue-gowned 'brethren'

men of standing is indicated by the fact that Harvey, the discoverer of the circulation of the blood, was its physician for over thirty years from early in the next century; but 'Bart's' did not develop as a medical school for another hundred years. Bethlehem Hospital was used, as it had always been, for the sick in mind, a class of unfortunates in whom the Elizabethans, as their drama attests, were deeply interested. Music, darkened rooms, low diet and the inevitable whip in cases of violence, were the stock treatment, but already the infamous practice of treating the fifty or sixty inmates of Bethlehem, or Bedlam, as a peep-show for the curious was making its appearance.

Unhappily Bedlam was chronically under-endowed. Christ's Hospital, on an old friary site, was for derelict children; their education was treated so seriously that Christ's developed into a great public school. St. Thomas's, in Southwark, became a place of refuge for those unfit for work, while the royal palace of Bridewell was given over by Edward VI as a house of correction in which the idle and vicious could be reclaimed through the discipline of productive work. The main part of the running expenses of these institutions, considerably over £4,000 a year, was found by the citizens of London.

Other towns where the problem was pressing and the means to hand followed the lead of London, and several of them, including Lincoln, Ipswich, Cambridge and Norwich, began by making a careful census and classification of their own poor. None of them could do things quite on the London scale, in five distinct institutions, but they used what they had in the light of London's experience. Norwich was in 1565 presented by its dean and chapter with a 'hospital' which was initially employed to meet the most urgent problem, as its 'Bridewell'; after a few years an elaborate scheme was drawn up to deal with the other types of 'poor' either in this institution or at home. The children were placed in charge of 'select women' in each ward who taught them their rudiments and set them to productive tasks by which they could earn sixpence a week. Soon the streets were swept clear of beggars and it was reckoned that some £3,000 had been saved. Ipswich similarly

Christ's Hospital, Ipswich, with (on the left) Bridewell and grammar-school

Merchant Taylors' hall and alms-houses in the City of London 1599

built a hospital on a friary site, and used it as its St. Thomas's, Christ's and Bridewell rolled into one. Bristol, Reading and York were equally active; Lincoln's constructive effort rose to the erection in 1591 of what was in effect a municipal technical school.

So far as can be judged by a few examples, the treatment accorded to the inmates of these institutions, except Bedlam, was by no means inhumane. They had to work hard, of course: maybe from four on a summer morning (five in winter) to seven in the evenings; but that was not so very much longer than the upper-class schoolboy's working day. They were liable to floggings for misbehaviour, but so was the undergraduate. A sample bill of fare included for each inmate eight ounces of rye bread, a pint of porridge, a quarter-pound of meat and a pint of beer daily, with cheese or a couple of herrings instead of meat on 'fish days': again not so very much below the undergraduate's fare. There seems little trace here of the principle underlying the nineteenth-century Poor Law, which Carlyle caustically summarised in the words: 'If paupers are made miserable, paupers will needs decline in multitude. It is a secret known to all rat-catchers.'

Small towns and rural parishes could not provide institutions of brick and mortar, but they tried to achieve the same effects in a less ambitious way. Their Bridewell might be just a temporary lock-up where vagrants could be lodged under guard overnight till they were passed on to the next parish; for although it was not until Charles II's reign that the Act of Settlement confined people to their own parishes unless they could show means of supporting themselves elsewhere, the whole system from Elizabeth's day was based on this idea of immobilising the poor. We had in fact our parochial immigration laws, with Bridewells as our Ellis Islands. The village counterpart of Christ's Hospital was a system of apprenticeship for all poor children. The apprentice of course boarded with his master, and if he was fortunate, as many were, he learned a good deal more than a trade; in fact apprenticeship was the working-class equivalent of serving as page in a gentle or noble household. It was not until the closing years of the eighteenth century that it was systematically degraded into a source of cheap factory labour, and children from London workhouses were bundled off by the cartload to Lancashire cotton mills to 'learn a useful trade' by machine-minding. In place of the endowed 'hospitals' of Norwich or Ipswich all that the small town or village could rise to was the provision of stocks of wool, flax or iron for the unemployed to work up in their own homes. Wherever possible existing endowments, supplemented by private alms, were used to finance these measures.

The time was now ripe for a more constructive national approach to the problem. It had become a little more manageable: enclosure in its more spectacular aspects was by now dying down, and the recoinage with which Elizabeth began her reign at least checked the wild rocketing of prices. Yet poverty was still widespread, and the northern rebellion of 1569 left a dismal trail behind it: 'I have not herd the complaynt so generall of povertye as yt nowe ys', wrote a man who had been travelling up and down Yorkshire a couple of years later. The very success of London's measures gave the problem a new twist, for in this same year, 1569, a tendency was noticed for the

Recoinage: coiners at work

destitute to drift there in quest of the loaves and fishes, much as the French unemployed flocked to Paris in the days of the National Workshops of 1848. Unless other regions caught up, London would be overwhelmed, just at a time when strenuous efforts were being made to check its immoderate growth. To strengthen the hands of local authorities in the country, a timid move was made in the direction of compulsory rates for poor relief: any parishioner reported as backward in voluntary contribution, after due remonstrance by the vicar and in the last resort the bishop, might be compelled to pay by order of the magistrates. This principle of compulsion had long since been adopted in London, when it found it could no longer meet its heavy commitments for the poor on a voluntary basis, and one or two provincial towns had followed suit. Its embodiment in this Act of 1563 was a foretaste of what happened more than three centuries later in the field of education, when Gladstone's government stepped in to fill the educational gap which had proved too great for voluntary effort.

The same year saw the formulation in the great Statute of Artificers of a code for those actually in work; it prescribed rules for apprenticeship on a national instead of a gild basis, and directed magistrates in each county to fix rates of wages for all grades of labour 'according to the plenty or scarcity of the time'. These two Acts prepared the way for the bolder measure of 1572, whose incidental effects on the acting profession and on the bardic order in Wales have already been considered. It was now possible to treat as a vagrant anyone who declined work at the rate of wages prescribed by the local magistrates, with the assurance that this was a wage based on actual living conditions. So the penalties were still severe, though not now so severe that the vagrant would be tempted to add highway robbery or murder to his offence, for good measure. To meet temporary distress, the principle of compulsion was carried still further in this Act by empowering justices where necessary to levy on householders of the parishes within their jurisdiction weekly assessments towards a parish fund for relief, and to compel substantial householders to administer this, without pay, in the interests of the poor, as paid officials were doing this in big towns. All this, however, still assumed that there were jobs waiting for those willing to work at reasonable rates; it needed a supplementary Act three years later to impose on all parishes the obligation of keeping stocks on which the poor could be set to work when no jobs were to be had. How the finished goods were to be disposed of in times of severe unemployment no one asked: presumably the charitable were to buy them up on the same principle that prompts us today to buy unwanted goods at a charity bazaar! The same spirit breathes in a letter from the privy council to the Somerset magistrates during a local recession of the cloth trade in 1586, couched in almost the same terms as Wolsey's letter to the clothiers nearly sixty years earlier.

Having thus built up the framework of a national system, parliament was now prepared to let matters rest. Other more exciting interests absorbed public attention, especially the struggle with Spain; and the privateering which followed the defeat of the Armada began to diffuse a general prosperity in which all classes shared in some degree. These were years of unbounded optimism, the effects of which were visible in almost every side of national life, from industry and investment to the arts. All the ruder was the awakening from this dream of a Golden Age when the old symptoms began to reappear from about 1594. The Spanish war had dragged on after the Armada without decisive results: it was beginning to look like stalemate, and a costly stalemate at that. The proposed expedition of 1594 was postponed again and again, and when at last it did sail in late summer of the next year, Drake and Hawkins both died at sea and the fleet was with difficulty rescued and brought home in 1596. Privateering was ceasing to pay: it is at this point that Thomas Myddelton withdraws his capital from these unproductive ventures and puts it into land.

Then, to make matters worse, for four successive summers from 1594 the English climate was on its worst behaviour. The first of them is memorably described in Titania's reproaches to Oberon, laying it all at the door of his jealous 'brawls':

> *the winds, piping to us in vain,*
> *As in revenge, have suck'd up from the sea*
> *Contagious fogs; which falling on the land*
> *Hath every pelting river made so proud*
> *That they have overborne their continents:*
> *The ox hath therefore stretch'd his yoke in vain,*
> *The ploughman lost his sweat, and the green corn*
> *Hath rotted ere his youth attain'd a beard;*
> *The fold stands empty in the drowned field,*
> *And crows are fatted with the murrion flock.*

Thomas Myddelton, who did a little farming in Lincolnshire as a side line, lost 280 sheep with foot-rot that year, involving him in a loss of nearly £180. Corn prices began to soar until they reached ten shillings a bushel in London and as much as eighteen shillings in remoter markets like Shrewsbury. This meant famine, which had begun to appear in several districts by 1596. Seven deaths from starvation occurred in the streets of Newcastle in December of that year, and as many as twenty-five in two successive months the following autumn. Food riots broke out in London and in Norfolk, and in Somerset the number of capital felonies in the single year 1596 rose as high as forty. In Bristol the corporation laid in a stock of corn and sold it in pecks and half-pecks to the poor, but when the stock was exhausted famine prices ruled again, and orders were given that every burgess with property should give one meal every day to the unemployed poor.

This was the background to the historic debate in the parliament of 1597 which brought so many distinguished members to their feet with rival plans, and issued in the comprehensive statute reissued with a few minor amendments in 1601, to remain the basis of our policy until the amending Act of 1834. It at least ensured that for the future no one need starve, and while establishing a pattern for the whole country, retained the principle of local responsibility and initiative to a sufficient degree to ensure elasticity. Probably it is one of the factors that have saved the country from social revolution; certainly it is one of the great legacies of the Elizabethan age, and for long it remained unique in Europe.

It did not by any means imply the abandonment of the medieval insistence on voluntary charity as one of the cardinal Christian virtues. The compulsive machinery was there in the background to ensure a national minimum in case of crises like that through which the country had just passed. In the normal parish in normal times it was not needed and not used. Even in Charles I's day enquiries from the privy council elicited the fact that Monmouthshire was the only Welsh county where the Act was invoked, and in remoter shires like Caernarvon no compulsory rates were levied till late in the eighteenth century. Private charity remained the first line of defence, and only exceptionally was it broken through. The allegation of decay of charity in the age of the Reformation, so often made by contemporaries and repeated by later critics, does not stand up to examination. Professor Jordan of Harvard, in a detailed study of wills and benefactions in London, Bristol and eight widely separated counties over the period 1480–1660, has shown conclusively that, so far from withering the charitable impulse, the Reformation stimulated it into new life after a period of decay following the golden days of the thirteenth century. Medieval hospitals still functioning were put under secular control and given a far firmer foundation by adequate endowment; and in little more than a generation after the monasteries were dissolved what they had formerly contributed towards the relief of poverty was more than made up, and far more effectively distributed, by private or civic benevolence.

The Elizabethan Poor Law did nothing to stem this tide of private charity; on the contrary it has been calculated that in the next generation more was bequeathed or given for this purpose than in the four preceding generations; and what was given was no longer narrowly local but nation-wide in effect— in fact Professor Jordan goes so far as to make this one of the factors in creating that sense of national unity which is one of the triumphs of the Elizabethan age. What did suffer was the endowment of worship. The prejudice in favour of plainer churches and plainer worship and against the endowment of perpetual masses for the departed told heavily against the recovery of the high proportion of medieval charity allotted to devotional purposes, and the resources of the church were gravely weakened by it. This change in the direction of charitable effort had begun some years before the breach with Rome, and must rather be charged to the change of temper that helped to bring about the Reformation than reckoned among its effects. The laity did not fully awaken to what had happened till the next century, and the damage was never fully repaired. Although Elizabethan charity was fervently religious in impulse, it was almost purely secular in its effects.

Further Reading

W. K. Jordan, *Philanthropy in England. 1480–1660*, 1959.
E. M. Leonard, *The Early History of English Poor Relief*, 1900.

IX

Travel at Home

It would probably be true to say that no Elizabethan ever travelled at home for the mere fun of it, except the 'rabblement' whose life was on the road. If respectable folk used the roads, it was simply to get somewhere, and they did not always succeed even in that. The word 'road' to Elizabethan ears did not mean a physical object, but a right: the right of the queen's subjects to pass from place to place within her dominions; and so long as the government ensured that such passage was possible, it had discharged its obligation. Since Roman times no one had *made* roads, nor did anyone seriously try to do so again till the days of Telford and Macadam. The only significant contribution of the middle ages to road policy had been a single clause in a statute of Edward I concerned with the maintenance of law and order; under this it was the obligation of lords of manors to cut down trees and undergrowth for two hundred feet on either side of the highway from one market town to another and to fill in any ditches 'whereby a man may lurk to do hurt', invoking if necessary the aid of 'the country'. There matters rested until just before Elizabeth came to the throne. Then an Act of 1555 shifted the obligation and re-defined 'the country'. Manor courts were ceasing to be effective, and one after another their duties were being transferred to the parish; road maintenance followed suit. Each parish was to elect its unpaid surveyor of highways for a term of one year, and he in turn had to see that for eight hours on each of four consecutive days all who held land in the parish should furnish carts, oxen or horses, and two labourers apiece, who with the help of all other able-bodied inhabitants (other than farm servants) should set to work on the road with their own spades, picks and mattocks. What is more striking even than the change in the incidence of duties is the change in the declared object of the Act. It is no longer solely a question of the lurker by the way-side; the preamble emphasises how the roads are 'both very noisom and tedious to travel in, and dangerous to all passengers and carriages'.

There is little evidence that the operation of the Act made them much less 'noisom and tedious'. All that was done by 'statute labour' was to hack down some of the undergrowth, throw stones into the largest holes and fill a few ruts with earth—with perhaps a little more attention to the road where the surveyor lived or the approaches to some important parishioner's house; for the obvious criterion was parochial, not national convenience, and a much-frequented highroad might receive no more attention than a country lane. The surveyor's main concern was to finish his year's turn of duty with as little friction as possible; and the county justices to whom he had to report would not concern themselves much

The Queen's dominions in 1590

Husband and wife travelling

unless they happened to be great travellers. The only money available for the job came from any fines imposed by the magistrates on those who refused duty. So it is not surprising that the duke of Wurtemburg describes a journey he took from Oxford to Cambridge in 1591 (through 'a villainous boggy and wild country, . . . very little inhabited and . . . nearly a waste') in little more favourable terms than those in which Dante's tutor had written of his progress from London to Oxford three hundred years earlier. One of the main northern exits from London was no more than a bridle path, and the western exit through Knightsbridge was a sea of mud in winter. When the queen herself travelled from Greenwich to Eltham it was by a muddy lane of irregular width winding through fields.

Luckily most of the English countryside, as we have seen, was devoid of hedge or fence, so it was easy for a traveller who found the road impassable at any point to turn aside into the fields and start a new track—maybe at the expense of the growing crops. This might in time become a new road, but it would need an Act of Parliament to close the old way; this happened to some of the worst roads of Kent and Sussex. Naturally wheeled vehicles were few. Men travelled on horseback, women and children in horse litters, or mounted behind their escorts. Pack-horses or pack-mules were the usual means of conveyance for goods over distances beyond the capacity of the farm cart. In the neighbourhood of London, the two universities, Windsor, Worcester, Exeter and a few other towns, long covered carriers' wagons were offering regular services by Elizabeth's time, usually over distances of fifteen miles or so, but occasionally much farther. From Oxford, by 1575, the university carrier left every Wednesday for London, to return the following Saturday, charging 2s. 4d. a hundredweight for bulky goods and a halfpenny a pound for small wares, with special rates for lutes and virginals. Another plied, less frequently, as far as Exeter. Even before this, Thomas Hobson of Cambridge had inherited a stable of eight horses and a cart, with which he set up as a university carrier until, over sixty years later, 'Death', in the words of Milton's undergraduate epitaph,

> Show'd him the room where he must lodge this night,
> Pull'd off his boots, and took away the light.

The carrier sometimes took aboard passengers who could not afford a horse and could not tackle the journey afoot, or who needed to travel with their goods. For the richer traveller, or rather for his womenfolk, the coach had been introduced from the Low Countries just before the reign began, but it took some time to win its way into favour; and no wonder, for it was unsprung, and its only superiority over the farmer's cart lay in the superstructure and the seats. A 'chariot' or 'whirlicote' had been used by royalty for state occasions as far back as Richard II's time, but the journeys in these were short, slow and stately. For longer journeys, at any speed, the new coach must have been sheer torture even to the well-padded Elizabethan, as the queen herself confided to the French ambassador at an audience in 1566, a few days after she had been 'knocked about' in her newly-acquired coach 'driven a little too fast'. A royal progress in which she had only once to leave her coach while 'hinds and the folk of the base sort' lifted it out of a rut was regarded as a memorable one. Being a good horsewoman, she wisely chose horseback as a rule; but on her progresses it might take as many as four hundred six-horse wagons to convey her goods! This, however, was largely because the houses she visited could not always supply the beds and other furniture needed by her numerous retinue.

An Elizabethan coach

John Stow, c. 1525–1605

Among the aristocracy the fashion of travel by coach is said to have been started by the last Fitzalan earl of Arundel, who died in 1580. Stow alleges in his *Survey* twenty years later that coaches have become 'so common, as there is neither distinction of time nor difference of person observed; for the world runs on wheels with many whose parents were glad to go on foot'. This can only have been for relatively short journeys in the immediate neighbourhood of London, where coaches were actually on hire at ten shillings a day early in the next reign. Farther afield they long remained a rarity. Sir Henry Sidney, lord president of Wales, caused a great sensation in Shrewsbury when in 1583 he drove into the town from his residence at Ludlow castle in his 'wagon' (which had brought his wife ahead of him), 'with hys trompeter blowynge, verey joyfull to behold and see'; but Sidney was prematurely aged, and perhaps unable to sit a horse. The wealthy Sir Thomas Hanmer, M.P. for Flintshire in 1593, probably owned the first coach in North Wales. On his death in 1619 he very properly left it to his widow, not his son; for coaches were still looked on as effeminate, so much so that an ineffectual attempt was made in 1601 to ban their use by men altogether. Hanmer's house lay in flat land where travel was relatively easy, and the Salusburys of Llewenny, the next neighbours to emulate him, were also on favourable terrain in the Conway valley. But it was long before the coach could negotiate the more mountainous regions. As late as James II's reign, when Lord Clarendon was sent to Ireland as lord lieutenant, he claimed to have 'introduced a new way of travelling' because he was able to send his goods all the way to Holyhead by coach instead of having to dismantle it for the more precipitous parts; even so he would not risk letting his family stay aboard!

Another form of danger, of course, still haunted the roads. 'Few venture to go alone in the country except in the middle of the day', a Venetian ambassador to Henry VII's court had reported, 'and fewer still in the town at night.' The danger from footpads and highwaymen had certainly diminished by the end of Elizabeth's reign, but the poet Churchyard was presenting rather too rosy a picture when he wrote in 1587 of Wales, one of the less settled parts of her majesty's dominions,

> *Ye may come there, beare purse of gold in hand,*
> *Or mightie bagges, of silver stuffed throwe,*
> *And no one man, dare touch your treasure now.*

At any rate the Shrewsbury drapers, when they went even as far as Oswestry to buy Welsh cloth, took no chances; they travelled in bands with weapons handy, fortified beforehand with prayers from the vicar of St. Alkmund's, who was paid £1 6s. 8d. a year for the service. After all, it was only three years before the reign began that the sheriff of Merioneth had been waylaid and slain by bandits. Even if the traveller escaped all the perils of the road, he could not hope to make any speed. The carriers leaving Rochester for London, whom Falstaff and his companions held up at Gad's Hill, had to start at two in the morning to reach their destination, a matter of thirty or forty miles, in 'time enough to go to bed with a candle'. Even a special messenger sent by the archbishop of Canterbury at four o'clock on a summer's afternoon of 1566, with urgent dispatches for Secretary Cecil, had to post through the night to reach his destination, sixty-three miles away, by eight next morning.

Riding in to market

Naturally the speediest transport on the roads was that provided by royal couriers. A dispatch from Greenwich to Stirling in Henry VIII's day was carried in six days, but news of the death of the last Tudor was conveyed from Richmond to James VI in Edinburgh in less than three. Such

145

speeds were abnormal; normally there was a good deal of difficulty in getting even official messages to their destination in
reasonable time. Until the next century the establishment here
of royal 'posts' lagged sadly behind what was provided on the
continent, and the mere private letter-writer had to make what
shifts he could: there was no public provision for him. At specified
inns on much-frequented ways the carriers of royal dispatches
could stop for the change of horses that must be made every
ten miles or so if speed was to be maintained; but except on the
vital roads to Dover, Plymouth or Southampton these relays
were kept in permanent readiness only in prolonged crises, and
then allowed to lapse on the score of expense.

The first long-distance posts to be organised were probably
those to Scotland; for Ireland they long remained spasmodic,
largely because of uncertainty as to the terminal port. Until
Elizabeth's reign it was generally Chester or Liverpool, but
both meant an undesirably long sea voyage. By 1561 it was
felt safe to establish posts through North Wales terminating
at Holyhead, by far the nearest point for Dublin; but there was
no assurance of a boat the other end, even if the horses were
ready, and this chain of posts terminating in a regular packet
boat was not finally established till 1599. There were also from
time to time posts for Bristol. When extraordinary despatch
was needed in some national crisis, extra posts had to be put on,
and a messenger was sent ahead warning the postmasters to
have the additional horses available on short notice. Anywhere
but on the recognised routes a royal messenger would have to
go armed with warrants to mayors and others authorising him
to impound horses at a penny a mile, if necessary unyoking
them from the plough. It is not surprising that complaints of
delay in delivery were frequent; they often gave useful cover for
local dilatoriness in carrying out the orders! Responsibility for
these arrangements rested with the master of the posts (later
known as the chief postmaster), the ancestor of our postmaster
general. It was an expensive service: in the year after the
Armada the queen was paying at the rate of 1s. 8d. a letter
for each stage over which it was carried, and the total cost was
some £5,000 a year. Private hire of post-horses at threepence

a mile for such as had occasion to travel 'post haste' was often provided both by official postmasters and by carriers: the 'choice' of horses offered by Hobson at Cambridge has become proverbial.

Probably the most constant users of the roads were these royal officials, couriers and poursuivants. As always, there were landlords and their agents travelling from estate to estate, but in place of Chaucer's friars and pardoners the roads were now aswarm with businessmen of one sort or another. Thomas Myddelton sold his cloth as far north as Edinburgh and as far west as Bristol, and he himself was frequently on horseback to visit his Lincolnshire farm, his Welsh estates or the ports where he collected customs for the crown and equipped vessels for raids on the Indies. Then of course there were the crowds who flocked to the annual fairs of Stourbridge or Bristol, King's Lynn or St. Bartholomew's in London, where householders for miles around restocked themselves for the next twelvemonth with the wares and produce, English or foreign, they could not raise for themselves or buy in the local market. Wrexham and Carmarthen performed the same service for buyers from North and South Wales respectively. The Canterbury pilgrims of the new age were men like Falstaff's victims on the road from Rochester: two carriers, one with bacon and ginger for Charing Cross, the other with

The Feathers Inn, Ludlow

live turkeys for the London market; on horseback a franklin of the Kentish weald, who might have served for one of Chaucer's company, had he not rashly announced that he had three hundred marks in gold with him, and a local official carrying tax money to the royal exchequer: all of them, with a few others, travelling in convoy for safety—and not finding it after all. The age of the commercial traveller had dawned, and the knights of the road, like so many other features of the age, were more secular than in Chaucer's day—in intent, though not necessarily, to judge by the *Canterbury Tales*, in conversation.

Much of their talk is about the inn, the Elizabethan substitute for the thirteenth-century hospice. They rail against its deficiencies, especially its sanitary deficiencies; and we are introduced to the seamier side of inn life in the conspiracy between its staff and the footpads. But foreign tributes to Elizabethan inns, and the comparisons made by travelled Englishmen, put them in a more favourable light. There was no doubt substance in the insular Harrison's boast that 'every man may use his inn as his own house in England', but his picture of innkeepers vying with each other 'for goodness of entertainment of their guests, . . . fineness and change of linen, furniture of bedding, beauty of rooms, service at the table, costliness of plate, strength of drink, variety of wines, or well using of horses' is perhaps a trifle highly-coloured; and his assurance that the larger towns provide 'twelve or sixteen such inns at the least', accommodating 'as many as three hundred guests', calls for a large pinch of salt. Contemporary inventories, however, suggest that the supply of both table linen and bed linen in a good inn did compare well with the supply in a private house of corresponding size, and was such as to allow of the frequent changes pictured by Harrison.

'One for the road'

If there were not quite as many substantial inns as Harrison suggests, there was no lack of taverns, alehouses and 'tipplers'. An obviously incomplete list drawn up in the 1570s gives a total of over sixteen thousand for the kingdom (not including Wales), ranging from Yorkshire's quota of nearly four thousand down to Ipswich's twenty-one: not far from twice as many per head as we have today. But this was before Ralegh received his monopoly of the right of granting licenses for the sale of sweet wines, which is estimated to have increased the number of licensed houses by some three hundred a year, and put anything from £800 to £2,000

The Falcon Tavern, London

into the courtier's pocket. The licensing of alehouses was one of the most important tasks of the county magistrates, with frequent prodding from the privy council. A government anxious to 'set the poor on work' was naturally concerned to keep within bounds these incitements to idleness and breeders of poverty: the fervent puritan Sir Francis Knollys, himself a privy councillor and a cousin of the queen, made the bright suggestion in the 1571 debate on the poor that a shilling should be levied on every alehouse keeper towards the upkeep of a local Bridewell. It was indeed not uncommon to squeeze out of the publican's profits money for any important local enterprise short of funds.

There was some concern too not only for the 'hinds and the folk of the base sort' who wasted their substance at the bar, but for the gentry who sat in one of the superior 'chambers' entertaining their friends to one or other of the foreign wines kept by the proprietor on licence from Ralegh, but not represented in the cellar of the manor house. For unscrupulous inn-keepers were apt to tempt young heirs by letting them run up a ruinous reckoning, and then to present paterfamilias with an uncalculated bill at an embarrassing moment in his fortunes. Yet it was not difficult to evade licensing restrictions in days when the mere hanging out of the traditional holly bush at fair time (an immemorial practice which survived to the dawn of the last century) was enough to invite thirsty travellers. There

149

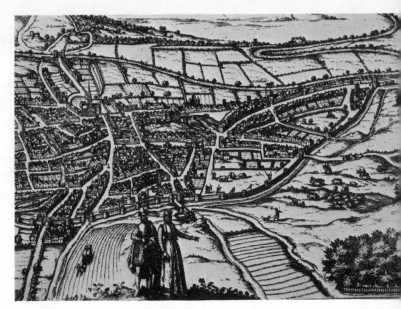

The approaches to Norwich, 1573

was no more physical difference between the cottage and the tavern than there was between the substantial inn and the small manor house—scarcely even the distinguishing Bear or Red Lion or Pelican, for such names were often attached to merchants' houses in London.

It was fortunate for the roads and for those who used them that they were not the only means of transport; English rivers still afforded an important alternative, and inland towns like Oxford and Cambridge, Norwich, York and Gloucester had something of the character of ports as well as markets. On the other hand most of the rivers were silting up, and, although there had been some activity in dredging and deepening during the fifteenth century on rivers like the Lea and the Severn, interest was not revived after the Wars of the Roses until the days of Charles II: it was not one of the developments into which Elizabethan capital went. Perhaps more important was the trade carried on round our coasts. Quite apart from the great export trade overseas to the continent, much of England was fed and fuelled by sea from other parts of the island. The most conspicuous case is the coal trade between Newcastle and London, but there was much carrying of corn by sea (when the boats were not stopped by local rioters or by government orders because of local shortages) from the better to the sparser corn-growing lands, when land transport was difficult. The Pembrokeshire cornlands often helped to feed both Bristol and the rocky shires of Snowdonia, and butter from the still unspoiled valleys of Glamorgan also found its way to Bristol and even to London by sea. There were plenty of travelled people in Elizabethan England; but those who travelled beyond the seas must be the subject of another chapter.

Further Reading

CONTEMPORARY

W. B. Rye, *England as seen by Foreigners in the Days of Elizabeth and James I*, 1865.

LATER

W. Lewins, *Her Majesty's Mails*, 1865.

S. and B. Webb, *The Story of the King's Highway*, 1920.

X

Adventure Abroad

The Reformation is commonly held accountable for the insular-minded Englishman of continental tradition. There is an obvious basis of fact in the generalisation, but like most of its kind it embodies only a half-truth. One of the less attractive aspects of the Elizabethan state, one which gives it something of the character of the modern ideological police-state, is its hostility to foreign travel. At the beginning of the century increasing numbers of cultured Englishmen had caught the fashion of visiting Italy, the recognised centre of European culture, to study at its universities, to meet its great scholars, to admire its buildings and statues, sometimes to persuade Italian craftsmen to come back and execute some piece of work for them at home. But the very word 'Rome' now had an ill savour in England, and the infection of Italian religion and Italian morals had to be kept at bay. So those who wanted to travel in Italy—or indeed on the continent at all, since so much of it still owed allegiance to Rome—met with many obstacles. It was hard to get permission, to start with; the passport nuisance had begun. The would-be traveller had to reassure the government about his orthodoxy, and for those at an impressionable age—the generation whose goodwill was essential to the continuance of the Elizabethan order in church and state—a particularly good case had to be made out. The traveller must also find sureties for his conduct abroad and his return on the expiry of his licence. Such licences were very sparingly given. The total for the seven years 1572–8, for example, was only sixty, the maximum for any one year being two dozen. So the Grand Tour could not yet become, as it was to be later, a normal part of a gentleman's education.

Superficially the Elizabethan 'license to pass beyond seas' bore some resemblance to the passport of a generation ago: a narrow strip of parchment about eighteen inches by eight, but unfolded and without the familiar hard cover, since Elizabethans lacked the commodity of pockets. Its purpose, however, was quite different. The main job was to get the would-be traveller safely out of the country, past over-zealous officials who might hold him up, and to protect his property, his family and his sureties while he was away. Once he crossed the seas, unless he was on government business, he must fend for himself. And there were many perils to dog his steps, other than the normal hazards of travel in a strange land. There were always spies abroad: sometimes agents of the government, more often free-lance informers who hoped to turn a dubiously honest penny by denouncing prominent travellers for attending mass or consorting with papists, or just for incautious words about the queen's government or her enemies abroad. Visitors were known to cut short their tours on hearing that spies were on their track. When they recorded their impressions they were careful to lay more stress on antiquities than on contemporary developments, even in art (except secular architecture), and most of them made great parade of their abhorrence of the popish practices they met.

To offset this narrowing of the horizon there were the zealous young students who went to Douay or Rome to prepare themselves, with certain loss of their estates and in the end deadly risk to their lives, for the mission of re-converting their countrymen; and at the opposite pole our new friendships with the protestant peoples of northern Europe, fostered by the Marian exiles and culminating in the uneasy comradeship-in-arms of the Dutch Revolt.

Yet there had never been a time when so many Englishmen from all parts of the realm had breathed foreign air or sailed the seven seas as during those last twenty years of Elizabeth's reign, when we were fighting on several fronts a war for survival. Year after year expeditionary forces were raised from far and wide to cross the Channel or the Atlantic or at least the Irish Sea, for service abroad which might last long enough for them to pick up some of the language or even to bring home a foreign bride. This was a very different matter from the short and sharp campaigns of the Hundred Years' War or Henry VIII's tinsel triumphs in France. Between 1584 and the end of the reign London and Kent alone sent well over eleven thousand soldiers to France and the Netherlands. This was by far the highest contribution, but levies averaging over five thousand a year in all were sent from every part of the country except the four northern shires, North Wales (including Radnor) and Worcestershire. Those that came off lightly in respect of continental service made up for it in Ireland, which was to that generation almost as foreign as France: North Wales, for example, sent over four thousand men there during the critical years and Worcestershire over a thousand, while Yorkshire, which contributed only eight hundred to the European campaigns, raised eighteen hundred for Ireland. On the other

The English in Ireland: Sir Henry Sidney, the Lord Deputy, setting out from Dublin Castle

English troops storming a castle

hand the Scottish marches were still not deemed safe enough to allow the northern shires to be denuded of troops for either field of conflict. Apart from official levies, volunteer contingents were raised up and down the country by captains of local influence whose able-bodied tenants and dependants went with them as a matter of course. The impact must have been something like what we saw in the 'twenties of the present century, when another generation of Englishmen had also experienced for the first time in living memory a continental war making heavy demands on civilian man-power, and every football ground and barber's shop echoed with the chatter of young men, never before out of their own villages, who referred casually to places with unpronounceable names and larded their conversation with pidgin French.

Elizabethan military service had another adventurous aspect besides travel abroad, for during the reign gunpowder won its final victory over the bow and arrow. Heavy artillery had of course been used, though not very effectively, for more than two hundred years, but the hand gun was a newcomer and suspect. Experienced soldiers were naturally loth to give up a weapon that could be made cheaply from our native yew and goose-feather by craftsmen of hereditary skill, and wielded by bowmen of the breed that had won us our great victories in

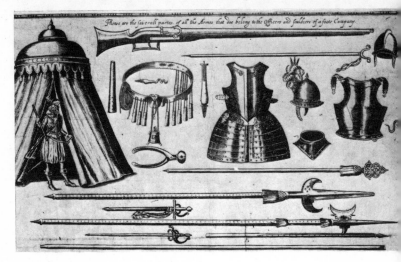

Elizabethan weapons

France: least of all for a contraption as liable to cause casualties
among friends as foes, increasing the cost of military equipment
by at least fifty per cent and leaving us dependent on foreign
supplies of powder. When the London trainbands tried out the
new weapon in Queen Mary's time many 'brake their pieces'
in firing them, others suffered burns, or in trying to avoid them
averted their heads and missed their aim: not an encouraging
experience. And so treatises in favour of the traditional weapon
were still being published by military writers of repute till
nearly the end of the reign.

Its rival, however, had been adopted by the leading power of
Europe, now our deadly foe; 'God forbid', wrote Sir Roger
Williams, the supposed original of Fluellen, in 1590, 'we
should try our bows with their muskets and calivers'; he even
claimed that '500 musketeers are more serviceable than 1,500
bowmen'. The advice had been anticipated in 1588, when recruits
levied in Wales for Ireland were suddenly ordered to change
their bows for muskets to meet an expected landing from the
Spanish armada. In the European campaigns the company of
bowmen which Leicester took out to the Netherlands in 1585
found no successors, and by the end of the century every
infantry company included a majority of musketeers and

calivermen, the rest being made up of halberdiers and pikemen. Firearms had won. Archery retained an honourable place among warlike exercises, but ceased to have any real military significance; the gunsmith's craft began to usurp the place of the bowyer's, and the perilous shortage of powder in the Armada fight forced us to find ways and means of manufacturing it at home, creating yet another new industry and leaving us dependent on the foreigner only for our sulphur supplies, for which, in the absence of natural deposits, our knowledge of chemistry was not yet adequate.

Adventure at sea naturally touched a narrower section of the community. The total sea-going population, even including the coastal shippers and the Thames wherrymen, was hardly equal to a quarter of the numbers actively engaged in oversea military service, and it was in the main concentrated round the seaports. On the other hand, the extension of trade had brought many a small inland town into contact with the ports through the apprenticeship of its sons to an exporter of London or Bristol or Chester. Sent in charge of a cargo abroad, these youngsters would learn the way of the sea or of the more distant oceans, and eventually, perhaps, find themselves picked as experienced mariners to sail on less peaceable missions with Drake or Hawkins or Frobisher. Most of them remained in contact with relatives in their home town, many came back to revisit it or even to settle down; and in this way knowledge of strange new lands and savage peoples filtered through, and slowly began to replace the fabulous folk-tales, handed down from medieval times or earlier, which had been the sum-total of their fathers' knowledge of remote lands. It was not long since men had believed that if they ventured beyond coastal waters or inland seas they might at any moment be sucked down into bottomless whirlpools, or cast ashore on islands of demons, or precipitated into Hades

A merchant ship

157

A wreck at sea

itself; many went on believing it in the next century. That men were prepared in such numbers to face these deadly risks, and that having done so they found so much of the lore of their fathers to be no more than old wives' fables, was the greatest revolution of the age: something far more radical, even if fewer shared in the direct experience, than a mere acquaintance with European lands or knowledge of the mysterious ways of gunpowder.

It all began earlier in the century. Coal-ships of Durham and Tyneside started looking farther afield than London to find markets in the Netherlands; even the little vessels carrying coal or corn from South Wales across the Bristol Channel followed their example and ventured to the coast of France. Merchant-adventurers of London or Bristol, encouraged by government policy, took their own ships to the ports of northern Europe, and south into the Mediterranean, for the wares formerly brought here by Hanseatic or Venetian merchants; and the Mediterranean trade, blocked for a time by the Turkish advance, was recovered by the daring of our own Turkey merchants, organised from 1581 in their Levant Company. Then again fishermen of Cornwall and Devon followed in the wake of Cabot, and after him Gilbert, to the Newfoundland banks in search of cod, and the herring fleets of East Anglia pursued the temperamental herring beyond the accustomed coastal waters, developing Yarmouth into a sizeable port. These crews and these vessels were the nurseries and the raw material of the crews that sailed the world and attacked

An Elizabethan galleon

the Spanish Main with Drake and Cavendish, Hawkins and Frobisher, and that saved our own coasts from invasion. Drake himself, as a recent historian of the navy puts it, was just 'a merchant seaman commissioned by the Crown in a crisis', and spent most of his life on private seagoing ventures; but he also developed a genius for naval strategy which brought him in line with the Raleghs and Grenvilles and Gilberts who belonged to the same social group as those who led our armies. They were, in fact, known as 'generals', not admirals, and they returned to their usual life ashore when the voyage was over. In this way Drake and the navy he helped to create were a great unifying force; when he insisted that the 'gentlemen' aboard must 'haul and draw with the mariners', he was welding together two traditions and two sections of the community no less than the playwrights who grafted classic conceptions of the drama or the architects who grafted Flemish or Italian novelties on to our native folk traditions. In this lay one of the chief elements of greatness in Elizabethan England.

The mariner had perforce to learn his job at sea, but some attempt was made to train the army recruit before he went into action, especially, of course, in the use of firearms; before the end of the reign the soldier unversed in this was regarded as untrained. It was reckoned in 1591 that of some hundred thousand men called up (mainly, of course, for home defence), rather less than half were trained and equipped. The most forward region was always the city of London. Stow speaks with

Drill-movements with the musket and pike

pride of the parades and manœuvres of the city trainbands;
to others the 'fat and greasy citizens' learning the art of war
were as diverting a spectacle as a Jorrocks or a John Gilpin
were to later generations. But for soldier and sailor alike it was
in the stress of action under experienced and trusted leaders
that 'ragged regiments of common rogues' were turned into
the human material that won immortal glory for the reign on
sea and land. Drake's confession in the course of his voyage

The funeral of Sir Philip Sidney at Arnhem, following his death at Zutphen in 1586

round the world, 'I have taken in hand that I know not
in the world how to go through withal', has a ring characteristic
of the age; but even more characteristic is the fact that he
did 'go through withal'.

Indeed the spirit of adventure which we have learned to
associate with the first Elizabethan age was rather a consequence
than a cause of the stirring events of the reign; it was a response
to a new challenge, and a response that would not have been
evoked without inspiring leadership. Mouldy, Feeble, Bullcalf
and Wart, Elizabethan recruits transplanted by Shakespeare
into the Hundred Years' War, show little enough of any thirst

for adventure; so, for that matter, do their real-life counterparts in the records of the reign. The gentlemen-captains who
volunteered for service, sometimes from religious conviction,
sometimes just to complete the education of a gentleman, and
roped in tenants and dependants bound to them by ancient
loyalties, were well enough before 1585. The latter type
generally served under Spain, whose armies then afforded the
best military academy in Europe; the idealists more often helped
the Dutch, though cases were not unknown of volunteers who
from religious conviction deserted the Dutch service for that of
Spain, like the regiment recruited by Sir William Stanley in
Cheshire and North Wales which betrayed Deventer to Spain
in 1586. Some remained in the Spanish service; others, becoming disgruntled with so unreliable a paymaster, transferred
their allegiance to the earl of Essex. But once we had openly
entered the continental struggle, the military needs of the
country soon outstripped such modes of recruitment, and we
had to rely mainly on random conscription at the discretion of
the lords lieutenant and their deputies and agents, with its
endless openings for graft and evasion.

Desertion on the way to the ports became common, and in
face of local sympathy and the absence
of any approach to an adequate police
force it was usually impossible to bring
the miscreants back to the colours. The
captains were not too worried, since
by a little judicious jugglery they could
often keep the deserters on the pay-roll
and pocket the pay; so most units were
chronically under strength. Over a
hundred men ran away from a Hampshire levy of 1600, and not one could
be rediscovered. Here the port of em-
barkation was close at hand; the case
was worse in a wild and mountainous
country like Snowdonia, where Chester
was the nearest port, and escape and
concealment were easy. Sir John Wynn

A pikeman drilling

161

complained in 1598 that recruits were taking to their heels wholesale on a rumour that they were to be drafted to the continent; yet the Irish service was so dreaded that men would 'venture any imprisonment' to escape it. It should be added that Sir John himself did not set an inspiring example: bent though he was on being everything a territorial magnate of his standing should be, he had answered an invitation from Leicester to serve under him in the Netherlands in 1585 by producing an impressive catalogue of his ailments! The unemployed and vagrants, sometimes even convicts, were swept into the forces in droves, if only to be rid of them, until military commanders began to jib against such unpromising material, and in response the practice was officially discouraged towards the end of the reign. The navy was more fortunate here: it could draw on a nucleus of experienced seamen, and its need for man-power could be satisfied without indiscriminate impressment; besides, it was not so easy to desert at sea!

On a par with the backwardness of recruits, and doubtless contributing to it, was the knavery of the captains and contractors on whom they depended for their pay, their rations, their clothing, their very powder and shot. Complaints of graft at all levels under each of these headings are incessant. It was when he felt, or knew, that he was being cheated over pay or rations that the soldier or sailor (then as always) was most ready for mutiny or plunder, and the elaborate and enlightened codes of military conduct laid down by commanders like Leicester or Essex or Hawkins became no more than pious aspirations. The soldier's nominal pay was about eightpence a day, but pay days were rare and meanwhile he had to make do with periodic advances on account, which rarely caught up with his arrears after the numerous leakages and deductions; it was Sir John Hawkins who raised the seaman's wage from 6s 8d. to 10s. a month, and, for a time at least, brought some honesty into the administration. Rations on paper were reasonable enough: the sailor was supposed to have a pound of biscuit and a gallon of beer a day, with a pound of salt meat four days a week and fish on the other three; the soldier's rations, which were included in his wages, ran on much the same lines, except that for him a daily ration of butter and cheese and

A fight at sea

sometimes vegetables (so sadly lacking at sea) was practicable, while meat or fish might come only once a week, washed down by a less generous beer allowance which could be supplemented locally by other drinks. But these rations often existed on paper only; then the soldier had to 'live on the country' as best he could, while the seaman, whose chief trouble was that the food went bad and the beer turned sour, just had to starve. No wonder disease carried off as many fighters as enemy action; and the neglect of the sick was a constant subject of complaint by the commanders.

The government did its best to investigate and remedy complaints of this sort when they reached it, and in the course of the war it gradually insinuated its own officials to keep an eye on recruitment and transport, made its own contracts over clothing and food, and forced the counties to make provision for their own disabled warriors; but lack of an adequate war chest hampered it at every turn, and its underpaid officials were always tempted to recoup themselves at the expense of the forces. In the navy the efforts of Hawkins from 1578 onwards produced a machine that creaked but worked; in the army the government was still fumbling to the end of the reign—and long after.

Like master, like man. With so much corruption and graft at the top pure patriotism could hardly be expected of the rank and file. 'We find it in daily experience', lamented Ralegh—himself by no means indifferent to the lure of gold—'that all discourses of magnanimity, or national virtue, or religion, or liberty, and whatsoever else hath been wont to move and encourage virtuous men, hath no force at all with the common soldier, in comparison with spoils and riches.' It was this lust for gold, the product of the sudden expansion of commerce beginning in the later middle ages and now reaching its apogee, that bedevilled Elizabethan public life at every turn: government, the church, the fighting forces, even exploration. It left its mark on Ralegh's own experiment in colonisation: what his settlers, and many that followed, looked for was quick riches like those that fell into the lap of Spain from the mines of South America. It cut short Frobisher's quest of a north-west passage in 1576–8, because the explorers found, on what was meant to be a temporary landing, quantities of a black stone believed, mistakenly, to be gold ore, and devoted their efforts on the two succeeding expeditions to an ill-conceived and (inevitably) quarrelsome effort to exploit it, clean forgetting their first intention. The scenes of pillage when the *Madre de Dios*, the

The first English landing in Virginia, 1584

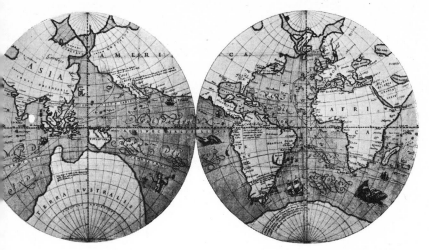

The circumnavigations of Drake and Cavendish

richest prize of the war, was brought into port in 1592 are a distressing foil to the stirring saga of her capture at sea.

It was well that there were men of the calibre of a Drake or a Roger Williams to give direction and discipline to the greedy restlessness of the age, and below them volunteer captains of ships or of infantry who entered the struggle in something of the spirit of Cromwell's Ironsides. In this way the Reformation opened out new and boundless horizons to balance its narrowing effect in other directions, and helped Englishmen of the age to face them with a sense of purpose whose very fanaticism was some offset to the pervasive gold-lust. It was one of the many paradoxes of the time that men by no means innocent themselves of its prevailing vice of greed were able to blend with it a burning patriotism and idealism, an unflinching hardihood and love of adventure, inspiring the motley elements under their command to incredible feats in exploring unknown oceans and facing impossible odds on sea and land. By their means immortal legends were created, like the epic folly of the *Revenge*'s 'fight of the one and the fifty-three', or, even more characteristic perhaps, that of the 'five tall and stoute shippes' of London 'intending onely a merchants voyage' which in 1586 fell in with eleven Spanish galleys in the Mediterranean, and drove them off, crippled, after a running fight of five hours. They were

165

legends that not only fired the blood of that generation but enriched the national heritage right down to the days of Dunkirk and the Battle of Britain.

Further Reading

C. G. Cruikshank, *Elizabeth's Army*, 1946.

C. Lloyd, *The Nation and the Navy* (illustrated), 1954.

A. L. Rowse, *The Expansion of Elizabethan England* (illustrated), 1954.

Index

INDEX